T0156549

Poetic Art

A wide assortment of colorful poems

by

George S. Hanna

with the help of Martin E. Hanna

iUniverse, Inc.
New York   Bloomington

Poetic Art

The Poetic Art

It's my joy to put ideas into verse,
in hopes of creating some priceless works.
I have chosen to use the poetic art,
since it really has the power to move the heart.
I recognize that the greatest power is spiritual,
and I intend to use this power to reach people.
The poetic art is the form of art I use
to express my beliefs any way I choose.
I have a very broad and large belief system –
one based on the Bible, not on humanism.
Through poetry, I try to lead blind souls to the Light,
and to reveal a vision of the future so bright.
Through poetry, I hope to inspire young people
to lift up their thoughts to a higher level;
I hope to challenge every girl and every young man –
with thoughts of inspiration – to reach as high as they can.
There is knowledge given only by the Holy Spirit,
and I want to be one of those who reveals it.
There is great and hidden truth which God has shown
in the Bible, which still remains unknown.
There is truth that has not been taught
by the humanistic school of thought.
These are some of the things I wish to impart
through the words in a book of poetic art.

Poems of Inspiration

The Beauty of Living

Welcome each new day as a new beginning,
and another chance to enjoy the beauty of living.
Don't accept the ugliness of life. Flee it.
Life has beauty, but few can see it.
One thing you have yet to discover
is the joy of being a blessing to others.
With pure love in your heart, you will.
Pure love for others could fill
every day you live with joy.
The beauty of life is there for you to enjoy.
But first you must plan and labor,
that you may turn things around in your favor.
Things wrong must not remain. Remove them.
And you must work to overcome every problem,
then you may enjoy the beauty of living.

I'm Free

I tear myself loose and get away
to be in the forest alone with God each day.
There is no wall to hold me in.
Gone is the nightmare I used to be in.
I run into the woods and leap and bound,
because God has turned my life around.
I'm going to live a life that's fulfilling and fun!
A total transformation has begun,
and I owe it all to the One
who has burst the bonds that held me.
Now I'm free to live victoriously!
Now I'm free of the bad emotions I used to carry.
Now I'm free to do the great things I want to do!
I'm free to stand up for what I believe is true,
and to express my beliefs the way I want to,
without fear of what people might say.
Like a bird in the dawn of a glorious day,
I could spread my wings and soar away!

Happiness

It is the hope of each new day
to get everything going my way,
and to see all my efforts turn out.
When they do, that's what I get happy about.
What is happiness to you?

Is it the hope of each new day?
Is it to live your life your own way?
Is it to share that ideal love
which you have always dreamed of?
What is happiness to you?

Is it to live your highest dream of success,
and to have all your days filled with promise?
To fall in love and acquire a mate,
someone you would always appreciate?
What is happiness to you?

Is it to do all of the things you want to do,
and to see your efforts amount to something?
Is that what makes your soul leap up on wing?
Is that what happiness is to you?

To me, it's in a love that is lasting and true.
It's shown in the songs we sing, and in the things we do.
It's when love and success are not a fantasy,
but a glorious reality!
It just makes your world look so bright
when you have love and success in your life.

To One In Search of Happiness

One does not forget so easily
the things which make one happy.
To attain self-glory will not do it. And you know
to attain success without God is just hollow.
All of your efforts were for nothing,
and the color of your life is fading.
You need to know what would make you happy,
and how you can get your life back into harmony.
You've got to have the hope of each new day;
you've got to be free to live life the right way.
Your emotional well-being depends
on having real love and real friends.
Just don't let anyone hurt you or turn you around.
Don't let anything or anyone bring you down.
If you can rise above a sad refrain,
then happiness is possible for you to attain.
But to attain happiness,
first you must ask and get God's forgiveness.
Then you must serve Him and show love to others a lot.
This brings real happiness; serving the devil does not.

How To Find Happiness

Many people want to know how they can
discover the joy of living again.
If you're filled with grief and sadness,
what could give you some real happiness?

First of all, Love!

It's one of the basic human needs.
It causes us to do unselfish deeds.
Love will create a desire to give,
to help, to heal, and to forgive.
When you're down, love can lift you like nothing else could.
Love is the highest motive for doing good.
And if you want it to motivate you,
then there really is something you can do.
Every day look for ways to be kind and loving.
If you do this, your emotional state will start improving.
Christ commanded us to love, because
of all the good it really does.
Love can fill your whole day with its glory.
Just speak with love to others and see.
Your most loving thoughts should be spoken.
With just one act of love, the spell of sadness is broken.
It really makes a difference what you say,
and how you live your life each day.

Second, using your talents!

If your life seems to have lost it's meaning,
then I have the solution you are seeking.
Meaning to your life will be restored
if you use your talents to serve the Lord.
Then joy will return, and hope will be restored.
Try to use your talents every day
to glorify God in some way.
It will cause a dream to come alive,
and you'll feel the excitement start to rise.
Pursuing a dream, and the pure love we give,
are part of what makes life worthwhile to live.
If you have neither, you can't be at your best,
and you have strong reason to be depressed.
Then you should kneel down to the Great King,
requesting of Him a new beginning.
But you must leave the dark side of life behind,
that the light of life may begin to shine.
if you do this, your dream will come alive again,
and you'll be happier than you've ever been!
Don't give up. Begin again today
with hope for a happier day.
Your heart will burst forth into song
when that beautiful day will dawn!

Show Love

So sad and empty is a life without love.
So many hate and hurt others just for fun,
and some don't know how to show love to anyone.
In a world so full of hate and evil,
we have the ability to love people.
And it pleases God when we show
love and kindness everywhere we go.
Show love to some of those you meet.
Lift up those who daily face defeat.
And express your most loving thoughts
before the opportunity to do so is lost.
Show love to bless others, so that their joy may be full.
You can show love in ways that are just beautiful!
You can brighten up someone's day,
or be a blessing in a special way.
People need spiritual sunshine.
There is so much darkness.
And so deeply do people need love.
There is so much sadness.
You can be joy to someone who has no joy;
you can be a ray of hope to one who has no hope.
Ask yourself: What can I do for someone today
that will touch their heart in a meaningful way?
What can I do that will really help that person?
What can I do to show love or compassion?
If you love that person, find a way to let them know it.
When you really love somebody, you want to show it.
And you want to show your love
in the most beautiful way you can think of.
So be creative! Every day
just think up some special way
that you can show love to someone.
And if you do, you'll become a truly beautiful person.

Love Poems

Note To The Girl I Love

He who walks above in His high world
thinks of you, even though He is way above you.
He comes out of the clouds with a sky full
of love for you, and in rushes this lovely
feeling out of the blue! Like a spring
breeze from the sunniest clime, He is
here to bless you at this very time!

In your life, so many wonderful
things He will do to show you in more
ways that He loves you. And each time
He shows you something, some new
revelation it will bring.

Someday when you find success in
your true calling, then life will look
just as promising as the very first
day in June, and then your heart will
sing the prettiest tune!

Wherever you go in life, and whatever
you do, remember, you have God, and
God has you!

Dear Miss

Just for yourself, find something wonderful in this letter.
And after absorbing these thoughts, you will actually feel better!
I write this with love to surprise you in a real nice way,
and to scatter sunshine over you and your day.
If you feel like you're about to drown in a stormy sea,
with no land in sight as far as you can see;
and you are being tossed about and teardrops form,
maybe I could help you through the raging storm.
Before you go under, I come to your rescue.
I'm throwing you a lifeline for you to hold onto.
You're about to sink, so let this lift your sad heart.
Suddenly, the waves of sadness are stilled, the dark clouds depart,
and the sun comes out with the chirping of birds!
I know I can delight you and lift you merely with words!
Now who would believe that a few words can
suddenly make you happy again?

Dream Music

As the day fades into the setting sun,
that's when a song is softly sung.
That's when dream music lulls so softly,
and never loses its beauty.
Relax, dim the lights so softly,
and listen to the words of my melody.
It's something for you to dream upon
as peacefully as a picture of a lake with a swan.
The music is taking you there,
to that beautiful somewhere.
Through a meadow and forest you walk alone
as you step softly on your pathway home.
Once in a dream I met you there
in that beautiful somewhere.
Your loving words were spoken
softly with sincere emotion.
And as the beauty of your love was felt,
I was lifted in spirit to a heavenly realm.
You spoke to me softly as a whispered prayer.
I felt the beauty of your spirit. Did you feel a gentler air?

Something So Beautiful

Dear, something so beautiful could live
if we are unselfish enough to give.
Surely you would not laugh and deny
that a noble love is possible for you and I.
Oh just think! Something so glorious
is entirely possible between us.
If we share joy without delay,
it would be a springboard to a brighter day!
And something so beautiful would live
if we are unselfish enough to give.
Sincerely as a child holds out his hand,
trying to tell you what you don't understand,
I am trying to tell you something so beautiful.
And if these words capture what I feel,
then you'll know this beauty is real.

A Song of Joy

I think of you and suddenly I am caught
in the light of a most beautiful thought!
I can do something to show love in all its beauty!
Suddenly a song arises from within me
with feelings which soar heavenward.
I bring you this day the lilt of a songbird!
I have a song, and its melody flows from
the first day you smiled, to all days to come!
My attitude toward you remains
like the sun coming out after it rains.
To me, the glittering pot of gold at the rainbow's end
would be the joy of having you as my friend.
We create joy out of the good things we do.
So I'll do some good things to create joy for you!
I'd like to put my hand on your shoulder and say:
Let's see if we can make this your brightest day!

My Future

Success is coming my way.
I'm moving up more each day.
I get the sense of ascending higher.
I notice every day it's getting nicer.
I'm going up. You want to go with me,
and find out how exciting life can be?
Don't you know, with love, it is possible
to make your life really beautiful?

In the business world, planning is the key
to reaching a higher position in society.
And that's just what I intend to do
with a delightful girl like you!
I am putting you in my future plans.
I'm going to walk into my future with you in my hand.
As I work for my future, and work for a dream,
the vision of my future really begins to gleam!

Poems About Success

Hope

My life used to be filled with sorrow,
and life was a burden to bear.
I had no hope for tomorrow,
and I thought I'd end up nowhere.

I wake up to a bright new day.
So many things are going my way.
My new life has just begun.
The darkness is over.
**Promises of hope are shining in me
for the future.**

I've got so much to do, and no time to waste.
Success is sweet, and I like the taste.
I'm living in a whole new way.
Life is so promising today.

All sorrow is over,
and things couldn't be better.
The tears have gone
out of life forever.
**Promises of hope are shining in me
for the future.**

The Road To Your Future

You are ever turning back to the places of your past.
Now shouldn't you get on the road to your future fast?
So…get off the road to failure,
and get on the road to your future!
What's the use in going nowhere, man?
If you follow a well-thought-out plan,
you could really get somewhere;
and I'll tell you how to get there.
So here's the plan:
You've got what it takes to make it happen.
Now just put your faith into action,
'til you reach the brightest dream you can imagine!
Don't let that dream be covered by the dust of the past.
You've got to have the kind of success that will last.
You need to take the shortest route
to reach the heights you've dreamed about.
If you move out on faith, you'll get somewhere.
You are going to thank God once you get there.

You Can

With God's help, there's nothing you can't do.
You can achieve any goal you pursue.
Don't let your goal be held back by fear or doubt.
If you can believe it, you can bring it about.
To some people your plan does not seem workable,
but you'll accomplish something remarkable.
Then you'll go forward and prosper,
and turn your whole life into one of honor.
Your future will be lived in peace,
and your blessings will ever increase.
No matter how impossible it may seem,
you can live your highest dream!
Your highest dream has so much glory in it.
Don't wait around. It's time to begin it.
You can make your dream come true
by doing the very thing you love to do!
After you lift yourself out of poverty,
you can be the champion of your destiny!
You can make your life change entirely!
Change it to the way you want it to be.
With God's help, there's nothing you can't do.
You can achieve any goal you pursue!
You can work for that goal, and not leave out the fun.
That is the best way your success can be won.

A Better Life

It is in the heart of every man
to live the life he believes he can.
And there is a better life for you.
This big wide world lies before you.
A better life awaits you somewhere.
You can just feel new promise in the air,
and the sky itself seems to say:
Get excited over what you'll do today!
Do what you've always wanted to do,
and go where God is calling you.
Down the road of life, wherever your dream takes you,
there you should go; there a better life awaits you.
God may open the door, but you've got to walk through.
It leads to a whole new life for you.
So right now, accept the challenge before you!
This is a challenge fit for heroes, kings, and noblemen;
and you have been chosen to take your place among them.
Because you have succeeded in doing the best,
you are sure to rise above all the rest.
With your brilliance, you're unstoppable.
You're the man who can tackle the impossible.
Yet in all your enthusiasm to achieve,
you must not forget to live up to what you believe,
in order to have the Father's blessings.
It is He who inspires you to do great things.
Someone gifted as you with a desire for success,
should never settle for anything less.
You should not be satisfied with your mediocre lot.
You can have a better life than the one you've got.
Something greater than you can even imagine
will come into your life and make it happen.
To every life there is a way.
To every person there comes a day
when it's time to make a change.
So get all your plans re-arranged,
and rise to the challenge set before you!

No matter how out of reach success may seem for you,
you were born to attain something higher!
So work toward the dream that you desire.
All the inspiration you need God will give,
once you venture into the dream you wish to live.
When you do, then life will give you more joy and gladness.
You bring hope to this world of sadness.
With your love, you can make even the saddest heart sing.
With your faith, you can do the greatest of things.
Faith is the key to unlock the talents you hold.
But you must act on faith, and you must be bold.
Do you know what acting on faith can do?
It can make life turn out right for you.

How To Get a Better Life

How often do you wish you could
live a life that is honorable and good?
The life you live now: are you satisfied with it?
The good life can be yours, and man you can live it!
The Lord wants your life to be fulfilling.
If you don't like the life you're living,
give it up for one that's better.
Now imagine the kind of life you'll enter –
the career and the life you wish you had.
And that's the kind of life you really could have!
A career using your talents gives great rewards.
And if you use your talents to serve the Lord,
it will give you joy and inspiration
beyond your wildest imagination!
If you do the work you love to do, it's sure to be fun!
You've got just one life to live, so make it a good one.
You can have the good life; and there's no doubt,
if you've got a dream, you can bring it about!
Once you do, you can laugh off the blues.
With these ideas to work with, you just can't lose.
Why be a loser when you don't have to be?
Just make some changes in your personality,
and then turn your life around in your favor,
that you may avoid a life of failure.
For all your efforts, God will reward you richly,
and open the door to a bright new destiny!
Your life will be a wonder for the world to see.
Just think how exciting that's going to be!

The Life You Want

With God's help, you have the ability
to build your life the way you dream it could be.
This is the truth – take it or leave it.
I'll let you in on a little secret:
Success has a pattern, so why not use it?
If God's Word tells how to prosper, why refuse it?
What do you do with a failure mindset? You lose it!
If you know God wants success for you,
then consider yourself one of the lucky few.
So tell me, what is it you want, exactly?
If you want true success, well take it from me,
putting God first in your life is requisite.
But you must be wise; you must be with it.
You must answer your life's highest call,
whether your success will be grand or small.
You must be guided by a Divine light,
that you may follow the best path for your life.
You want to live the life you dream about.
But you must not leave the most important thing out.
And that's faith. Faith is an important factor
in reaching whatever in life you are after.
The life you want is possible to acquire,
but to reach that objective does require
careful planning, dedication, work, and self-control.
If you want a life of purpose, you've got to have a goal.
But a life without purpose: There's no meaning to it.
God has given you a mission, and only you can do it.
You'd better pull your thoughts together and form a plan,
that you may reach your goal the fastest way you can.
Perhaps enter a career that's exciting and fun,
or do what people thought couldn't be done.
Whatever you're inspired to do, that's okay,
as long as it would glorify God in some way.
You don't want to stay on the level you're at,
and you want to know how you can rise above that.
You can rise up higher if you're ready to find

a new life and put the old behind.
Take that new career: Can you see yourself in it,
living the life you want? Can you imagine it?
Through all the darkness of life, can you see
the dawn of your bright new destiny?

Advice For Young People

The way I see it, in this world
you've got to make your way.
You've got one chance in life.
Just don't throw it away.
A person with as much potential as you,
should be able to accomplish what you've set out to do.
When you take on life's challenge, laugh and make it fun.
But don't forget to invoke the help of the Highest One.
He speaks to your heart,
and lights up a dream within it.
You have a mission in life,
and now you must begin it.
Right now start planning for that brighter day!
Start planning to make success come your way!
Dream about the life you want.
And the more inspired you feel,
the more you'll work to make
that dream become real!
If you think a dream won't take you far,
just look across the distance to the brightest star.

Become Successful

I'd like to help you become successful, if I may,
before all your faith in the future slips away.
If you follow my suggestions to the letter,
the spirit of failure will leave your life forever.
What people say you can't do, that's just what you should do!
Brighten up the dim view they have of you.
You know your life could be a shining example
of applying principles to become successful.
The world loves a winner, and that's what you've got to be.
You've got the vision; you've got the ability –
the ability to become successful!
Don't put up with being bossed and pushed around.
Too long you have been beaten down.
The wicked laugh as they take your last dollar.
They're glad to see you suffer in squalor.
You could rise above financial disaster.
You could rise to the top of the social ladder.
They think they'll keep you down, but they will not!
Now's your chance to show them what you've got.

Become successful!

Build Your Dream

Within your lifetime, you have the ability
to build a dream, and make it a reality.
This is your life's highest call. Will you answer it?
That elusive dream can be real once you capture it.
I'll tell you how, but first consider why
most people don't choose to even try.
Just lack of faith is the reason
in almost every situation.
You see, faith is what determines the difference
between a life of failure and a life of significance.
And it really does matter a lot
what kind of faith you've got.
Faith is an important factor which seems to motivate
those who set out to accomplish something great.
And so what if you don't have the faith to make it happen?
You can develop faith through action,
like daily practice and preparation.
It doesn't take much, just a little bit every day
is all it takes to get things turned around your way.
It's going to be exciting to live a life of victory;
to earn a living using your gifts for God's glory.
You want to see how great this life can be!
To build a dream, and bring it into reality!
And so if you start building that dream, and keep God in it,
before long you'll be living that dream! Just imagine it!
Now it's your choice to pursue
the greatest thing that you can do.
If you really put your heart into it,
you'll find that you can do it;
no matter how unrealistic it may seem.
If you believe you can fulfill your dream,
then surely it can be done.
Acting on your faith will make it happen.
If you've had faith to achieve one great thing,
then you are ready to take on higher things.
Do you have no faith in that?

Ask yourself where your faith is at.
Although it may be hard for you to believe,
you can do something which no one else can achieve.
The power of God will enable
you to do what seems impossible.
But first, invest in your dream as much as possible.
If you do, then you'll progress forward fast,
and you'll see that dream fulfilled at last.

The Good Life

The American dream can be yours, too.
There's a new life waiting for you.
It's the brightest dream you can imagine,
and you're going to make it happen!

Right after your day of success arrives,
you will not have to struggle and strive.
Then you could free yourself from struggles and strife,
and that's what it takes to live the good life.

You can have the good life. I'll tell you how
you can be a winner starting now!
I heard you say, "I wish I was."
Well, then, don't do what the failure does.

You know what you do with failure?
You take it to a cliff and shove it over!
Leave behind the failure mindset.
That's what you must do to get…the good life.

You can have the good life, and there's no doubt
that there is a way for you to bring it about.
First, you turn things around in your favor.
Then you give your life a complete makeover:

New pursuit, new attitude, new image, new look.
If you really do it by The Book,
and glorify God and not yourself,
He will be happy to bless you with wealth.

Your success will surely be won
if you put your faith into action.
You can succeed if you believe you will.
Success could happen to you as well.

If you go against your fear and doubt,
and act on faith, you'll bring it about.
This is how it's going to happen,
and this is how it's going to be done!

Change Your Life

So many who fail end up ornery and bitter.
You know what? I think you could do better!
If you put forth all the effort it takes, you can.
But first, you've got to make a plan
to change your life for the better.

You could get everything you want in life,
but you've got to play your cards right.
Before God will give you all that you have wanted,
you must do what He has commanded,
in order to have that good success.
You should be working for this very purpose:
to change your life for the better.

You've got to take charge of your situation.
That requires faith, effort and determination.
You've got to give it all you've got,
if you want to make your life improve a lot.
You can make your life improve a great deal
after your highest dream becomes real.
With a dream in your heart, you could follow your star.
One with your abilities could really go far.
Right today, start your life anew.
Let your highest dream inspire you
to change your life for the better.

Have something to show for your life
when you face God in eternity.

Get Excited

For you to succeed in life is God's will,
because you have a destiny to fulfill.
You can't wait to see how great it's going to be!
Don't wait 'til the day you reach your destiny.
Praise God now with dance and song,
even before it comes along!
If you know He wants you to succeed,
then just ask Him for what you need.
When you get what you need to move ahead,
thank God for it, and get excited!
Get excited about what you're going to do!
With God's help, your highest dream will come true!
Right now get your dream to come alive!
Don't wait 'til the day you arrive.
Praise God now with dance and song,
even before it comes along!
Claim your success even before it's won!
Show up those who say it can't be done!
People don't even know what you can do
when you have God working through you!
He's going to help you carry out your grand endeavor.
You can't wait till the day you see it all come together!
Praise God now with dance and song,
even before it comes along!
All the dark clouds of failure will leave
when you get excited about what you're going to achieve!
If all this seems too awesome and grand,
that's how great it is when you have God in command!

Pep Talks
(Motivational Poems)

Charismatic Poem
(to recite in church)

Visitors, you may be afraid of what you might hear,
but you sure came to the right place when you came here!
If you expect to fall asleep, it ain't gonna happen!
Before the service is over, you'll be jumpin' and laughin'!
If you don't restrain yourself,
you'll have so much joy you won't contain yourself.
Should you really get all that excited?
If it would make you come alive, go ahead!
Get all excited! Get all excited!
You've just got to let go of your fear.
It's appropriate to show your excitement here.
As we worship together in one accord,
you may want to dance to the Lord.
If it would get you in the spirit,
and get you out of yourself, do it!
Get in the Spirit! Get in the Spirit!
Get in the Spirit of the Lord,
that your joy may be restored!
If you are led by the Spirit to rejoice,
don't be afraid to raise your voice
and shout, scream or sing with emotion.
If you express to God your love and devotion,
it will give you joy and gladness.
Claim the victory over sadness!
Claim the victory! Claim the victory!

We've Won!

We've won! Though Satan, our opponent, has cheated,
we know, praise God, he is now defeated!
In the game of life, we are the biggest winners!
Those who play on the opposing side are the losers.
They will lose in the very worst way
when they face God on Judgment Day.
Those of us on the side of the Savior
will win when the game of life is over.
We're the winners!
Though people put us down and make fun of us,
they are just jealous of our goodness.
Though people say "you're nothing," that's a lie.
We are sons and daughters of the Lord Most High.
He honors us, and we have infinite worth.
Just being born again gives us a noble birth.
As we serve God, we often
come up against opposition.
In every way he can, the devil tries to defeat us.
But as long as we stick with Jesus,
share His love, and keep from sin,
then the darkness can't possibly get in.
In the game of life, we win.
We've been winners from the day
we first turned to the Lord to pray.
We each have failed the mark, no matter how we tried,
till we came over on the Lord's side.
Now we're on the side of the Almighty,
and He's using us in the community.
We're on the side that's going to win,
because we accept Christ and reject sin.
We have won the highest love:
the favor of the Lord above.
We have won the highest prize:
Heaven itself, and a mansion in Paradise!

Our Mission

God's given each of us a mission
to accomplish for the King of Heaven.
Ignore those who say it can't be done.
God has given us a mission!
We just have to walk it out.
Now it's time to get excited about
the great things we're going to do!
Serving Him is the most exciting venture one could pursue.
When God reveals to you and I
some aspirations which are so high,
that's when we get excited about
the mission we're going to carry out.
Our mission is to offer salvation,
and to restore a fallen generation.
It's big enough to encompass
exciting new avenues of service,
which He inspires us to enter,
that we may serve Him better.
To God all praise and glory is due
for each great work He inspires us to do.
Part of our mission is to spread God's Word with love.
Pagans teach their word: Whose word are you assured of?
I say and they say, but what does God say?
Look into His Word and follow His way.
The truth is there for you to receive it,
but is it in your heart to believe it?
Believing bright new truth is like a bridge which we
cross over to a higher reality.
There is knowledge given by the Holy Spirit,
but it's only accepted by those who believe it.
Part of what you do not believe, really is true.
Someone could be right whose ideas are new to you.
Some ideas of ultimate worth
have a parallel not on this Earth,
because there's nothing earthly which can surpass the heavenly.
Today our mission is to Earth.

But our mission someday
will reach out to other worlds
beyond the Milky Way.

Personal Guidance

What A King Did For You

Somewhere in a far away land,
there's a King whose throne is forever.
Worlds are in His hand as so many bits of sand.
His power holds the Universe together.
He came from His realm on high
to save people just like you and I.
Imagine the height of the heavens – how high they are!
Who could have authority over every planet and every star?
That is something which only a god could do.
Only a god could reach across the stars for you.
Just think! The greatest person of all time
loves you with a love that is Divine.
He wants to bless you in a thousand ways,
and that's why we all should give Him praise.
Praise Him, because He died to pay the cost,
that He may save your soul from eternal loss.
It is so hard to think that One with love so great
was mocked and treated with cruelty and hate.
He placed His hands upon the cross to bleed,
and to take the punishment for every evil deed.
The entire Universe was under His control,
but He chose to die to save your soul.

His Love For You

Love is the greatest power in the Universe.
It's what brought a Savior down to Earth.
To save us, love compelled Him to die.
It is this love which we hold so high.
Throughout history there was never known
a greater love than the Son of God has shown.
You would not feel unimportant to Him,
if you would consider
that however vast the heavens are,
His love for you is bigger.
And no matter what you do,
never will His love dissolve.
You may have a problem
which only a god could solve.
He would help you with that,
if you ask for His help.
He cares for you more than
you care for yourself.
He sees all the good in you,
and all of your potential.
In His eyes, you are
someone really special.
You belong to Him and you are His.
See how wonderful His love really is?

His Love

Come and join with us in worship and prayer.
Open your heart to His love, and He'll be there.
For a moment be in holy silence,
and soon you'll feel His presence.
As far as your faith will allow,
Jesus comes to you quietly now.
His Spirit speaks to your spirit:
"I love you." Even the silence would say it.
Try to feel in this holy hour
His presence…His love…His power.
If His love is touching your spirit,
you will feel the beauty of it.
And you'll want to keep yourself
in His love, that He may
keep you close to Himself;
and you will always want it to be this way.
So walk with Him along life's pathway
every sunrise of every beautiful day.

Only a God

You try to be totally alive, living life to the fullest.
You try to be on top of everything, and to feel your best.
But when you feel down in your darkest hour,
only a god could uplift you with His power.
No matter how you fail Him, never will His love dissolve.
You may have a problem which *only a god* could solve.
You have but to call on Him in your time of need,
and He will speak up on your behalf, and intercede.
He would stand between you and death itself.
He's the one person you need above all else.
Against the whole world He would take your side,
because you are one of the people for whom He died.
His love for everyone was bigger than His own life.
When He died, the sun for a moment stopped shining her light.
Who would die, and then come back to life for you?
That's something which *only a god* could do.
Only a god who stands for truth like a megalith,
could defeat our last enemy, which is death.
Of all the men who ever lived, only one
went up against eternity and won!

Serve Him

We who are destined to a higher world,
are certainly held to a higher standard.
It's not enough to do good and to sing His praise,
we must also obey His Word and follow His ways.
He is the King we really enjoy serving.
Even though you don't feel worthy or deserving,
He will give you a place in Paradise.
Till then, you must keep your faith alive
by devoting your life to the most important things:
Follow a higher cause, and serve the King of Kings.
We who love this King in all His majesty
choose to serve Him in some capacity.
When you serve Him at your very best,
that's when you'll be your happiest.
He wants you to serve Him, because He needs you.
He wants you to follow wherever He leads you.
If you follow Him, a promising future you'll face.
But you've got to learn to use the power of faith.
You may not have the faith to move a mole hill,
but if you do the Lord's work, you are in His will.

Soon Life Will Be Past

Every day I look out my window
and over the horizon of long ago.
My thoughts go back to some pleasant memory,
as I reflect on how things used to be.
I remember the wonder of spring
when my heart first began to sing.
This life is so short.
Soon life will be past.
And what have I done
for God and for others that will last?

In the light of eternity, life is like a minute.
We've got a short span of time on this planet.
You may become great in a time of history,
and leave your footprints in eternity.
But like the waves rushing over the sands of the bay,
the footprints of your life will be washed away.
This life is so short.
Soon life will be past.
And what have you done
for God and for others that will last?

Little Bird

There once was a songbird chirping in the dawn
over the hills I used to wander on.
It seems so far away, yet it comes back so clear.
It comes back across the years.
In so many ways you've lost and failed.
In joyful flight a bird no longer sails.
But the little bird with broken wings
is found and cared for 'til he soars and sings.
Let God put your broken heart back together,
that your heart may sing with joy forever.
God comes to you through these words today
with compassion to take your hurts away.
And perhaps such simple words as these
will lift your spirit like birds lifted on the breeze.
God will care for you 'til the day you fly away to His Kingdom.
Then you'll soar above this world on the wings of freedom.

You and Your Ltitle Boat

As you sail away in your little boat out on the sea,
will you ever reach that island of beauty?
When your little boat is tossed about as teardrops form,
maybe I could help you through the raging storm.
The raging storms of life will come upon you,
so I'm throwing you a lifeline to hang on to.

When a storm arises, and your little boat
starts sinking and you can't stay afloat,
let the Lord lift you above the waves of sadness,
and bring you safely to the land of happiness.
On this bright hope you would float
as long as you let Him guide your little boat.

Before it drifts out of sight over the horizon,
let Him take the helm. He's your Captain.
Dear, if you do what He tells you to do,
the most wonderful things will happen to you.
You'll be carried upon the breeze to those peaceful shores,
then He will put joy in those pretty eyes of yours.

Jesus is Your Friend

(to be read to a child)

I want to talk with you about Him, if I may.
He is so important to your life each day.
He can actually hear and answer your prayers.
He wants to heal each little hurt, because He cares.
He who forgives and takes all the evil away,
will surely lead you in the right way.
He who loves you and keeps you from harm
is the true keeper of your heart.
He's concerned about your life in every detail.
He watches over you when you fail,
when you think you're worthless, and when you cry.
He alone understands you, what you do, and why.
And as long as you keep your heart harmonious with His,
you can see how wonderful He really is.
How can the lost see what He is like, except through
someone so loving and kind as you?
You belong to Heaven. But until you enter
that land of peace and joy forever,
follow Jesus in all that you do,
and it will lead to happiness for you.
He'll lead you into avenues of service,
and give your life a real purpose.
He'll lead you into avenues of love,
and bring you into a home prepared above.
You belong to Jesus, and you are His.
He wants to give you each blessing there is.
How wonderful it is to have Him as your guide.
And a friend – the One you follow
wherever life will take you; wherever in life you go.
For each of us needs a friend,
someone to lead us 'til the journey's end.

The Real You

I want to know the real you.
Take off the disguise.
Just the way you are
is beautiful in my eyes.
You are someone very special,
and you've got so much potential,
so you must learn how to use it.
Don't do what others do,
and then just excuse it.
Speaking with love,
I'm here to remind you
to put all that behind you.
Let your special qualities shine through,
because they make up the real you.
The true vision of yourself
is what I can see.
The real you – that's what
your God wants you to be.
Don't try to be something you're not.
Keep those special qualities
which you've got,
because they are what makes up you –

the real you!

Apostolic Word

God wants to know if you're going to go His way,
or if you'll let something else pull you away.
Tell Him what is your response.
When we go along with what God wants,
that's when we are victorious,
and that's when His light shines through us.
And this light is triumphant over darkness.
To you has been entrusted the sacred light,
because God has a wonderful plan for your life.
You may not see the purpose of His plan,
until you see the moving of His mighty hand.
But can you believe this very thing –
that His plan for your life is happening?
God has chosen to use you, as well as this writer,
and we each will make the whole world brighter!

Dear Young Person

There's something I'd like to talk with you about.
Did you know that God has your future all figured out?
Everything right now is so confusing to you,
and you don't know what your life is leading to,
or what field you should go into,
or what plans God has for you.
Your great talents could be used for the glory of God.
Read His Word, and find out what plans for you He's got.
In God's Word is something so fantastic,
that just a small verse would work like magic,
if applied in the proper way
in the life you live each day.
Obey what His Word tells you to do,
because He wants what's best for you.
So read His Word, and to the extent that you obey,
He will work in your life in a miraculous way.
So many possibilities are presented to you,
and you don't know what's best to do.
Ask God to show you. He sees the bigger picture.
Your small viewpoint is not the only view to consider.
You may only consider a few things,
but God considers everything
in deciding what is best to do,
and what is the very best thing for you.
Let Him help you guide and direct your life, because
you don't always know what's best for you, but He does.
And if you do what He tells you to do,
it will result in great happiness for you.

The Book

The most important subject of study
involves the Bible and human destiny.
Out of the sacred pages there will always shine
verses which awaken within us something Divine.
Gather inspiration from The Book.
That's not a source to overlook,
because The Book you should be reading
really does reveal life's greatest meaning,
and life's greatest challenges.
When we look into Bible passages,
we can be inspired to live by the loveliest ideals,
and to live by the truth which The Book reveals.
This truth is captured most skillfully by poets and sages.
And as we study the sacred pages,
we can be touched by a truth which is sublime.
We can apply it, and triumph over the sadness of a lifetime.

The Truth

Seek the truth and you will not be blind;
live the truth, and it will expand your mind.
Some people voice the truth, and voice their objection to fallacy.
But most turn their back on truth, due to fear, disbelief or apathy.
What kind of signal are we sending to our youth,
if we don't have the courage to stand up for the truth?
Let's speak the truth, in spite of how the God-haters react.
That Christ actually lived is an historical fact.
Let's be courageous enough to speak out
against anything we disagree about.
Don't make people think you agree using false pretenses.
A man of honor will tell the truth in spite of the consequences.
A courageous life is like a mountain projecting a vision of grandeur.
It takes a mountain of courage to stand for truth and to endure.
A mountain may crumble and wash into the sea,
but the truth will stand for all eternity.

A Piece of Wisdom

There's nothing better that a man can do
than to put in his life the things that are true.
If a man really lives by the truth,
he will have in his life the proof.
God will work with a righteous man,
but He will have no part of a fool's plan.
God commands – and His followers choose –
not to remain in the company of fools.
Away from them you should walk.
Mistakes are made by idle talk.
Those who complain about their meager lot
should rather thank God for what they've got.
Don't speak words which seal your fate.
You can change it with words of faith.
If you're going to speak, say something nice.
Look at others through the eyes of Christ.
And if we begin to bless, rather than curse,
could life become better on planet Earth?

Philosophy

Your Reality

We each will begin a perfect day
either in a negative or in a positive way.
Which of the two you accept becomes your reality.
Your belief or disbelief decides which it will be.
Those who don't live by the truth, live by an illusion.
It's getting so that people do not even know what's real,
and in their thinking there's much delusion.
Very few believe the truth which the Bible does reveal.
The majority live by their whims and the word of people,
instead of the Word of God and the truth that's eternal.
You may think the majority is right, but that's not true.
The majority is wrong on almost every spiritual issue.
You can live by the delusions and the mindset of the majority,
or you can live by the truth and the ideals of Christianity.
Which of the two you accept becomes your reality.

The Highest Truth

To all mankind I bring a message
and some wonderful new knowledge.
Understand not just the surface,
but the meaning beneath it.
You may understand it, but will you believe it?
Part of what you do not believe, really is true.
Someone could be right whose ideas are new to you.
I share my ideas to enlighten and to inspire,
and to help your thoughts reach higher.
I'll take your thoughts among the stars
of the colossal cosmos.
The highest truth can't be contained
within the minds of most.
To find the highest truth which men have sought,
you would have to enter a new dimension of thought.
To do this, one must interpret truth
<u>not</u> on a level that's limited and small,
but interpret truth in larger terms to encompass all.
Some things beyond your knowledge I will explain.
Some wonderful new ideas I will make plain,
that you may learn…

the highest truth.

Something More

Many people today are searching for
something missing in life; something more.
It's worth more than success in one's chosen endeavor,
for it is life's greatest intangible treasure.
Life's greatest treasure you could actually find!
It's worth more than diamonds and gold combined.
I'm saying this to help you see what you're really after.
It's something the mind of most can't quite capture.
All the world is searching for something
that does fulfill man's deepest longing.
It's the unconscious need of all who live –
something greater than this world can give,
yet without it, life is empty.
In order to be truly happy,
one must not live just for happiness, but for something more.
When you find it, you'll have the greatest thing to live for.
The greatest thing to live for! And finding it
would fulfill the longing of your spirit.
One who fulfills this longing discovers life's true meaning.
Life's true meaning: only that can fill the emptiness,
and you'll never by happy with anything less.
For life is hollow and empty indeed
when you have not the greatest thing you need.
This world can offer only the material,
and does not even recognize the spiritual.
But Heaven has something greater than this world can give,
and God can actually put it into the life you live.
You may think this is simply not true.
But there is something more for you.
There's a whole new dimension to life you have not yet explored!
Finding it is like finding life's lost chord.
Life's lost chord can actually be found!
When you find it, its effect on you will be profound.
Then suddenly you'll see life differently,
and your view of the world will change permanently.
It is what you perceive life to be

that creates your perception of reality.
But there's far more to life than what you perceive.
You see only a small part of what there is to believe.
Your view of life is only what you perceive it to be,
but there's a grander scheme of things which you do not see.
And you will only see the larger view
if you come into the new dimension which God has for you.
Come into the new dimension!
And your reality will be altered through Divine intervention.
God's Word will give you the true perception of reality,
if you abandon the shallow mindset of society;
and align your ideas up with Scripture,
in order to get the bigger picture.
Then God will give you the larger view
of what life is, and what He has for you.
You see, God has a grand and glorious plan
for the heavens, for the earth, and for man.
And when you become His, and answer to a higher call,
you will see that something really is behind it all –
something that links all things together.
And once you get it, you will keep it forever.

Poems To
The Unsaved

What You're Really After

You can see lonely people everywhere
searching for something that isn't there.
Something in life is missing which can't be replaced;
something important that was lost or misplaced.
You may search the world over
to find in life what you're after.
You may try
getting great wealth, a lot of thrills, and laughter,
but that will not satisfy
the deep, down longing for what you're after.
You may go from metaphysics to scientology,
to seeking answers in New Age philosophy.
But it's not there, and you won't find it
in the wrong places.
You have lost something which
nothing replaces.
You have lost your connection with your Creator,
and you can only get it back through the Mediator.
Through wrongdoing you became spiritually dead.
To the Source of Life you were disconnected.
But through Christ you can be revived, and you can
come alive with spiritual life again!

Tune In

Feel a longing, and you don't know why?
Like nothing of this world can satisfy.
Separation from God caused that.
To return to God is the answer.
Dropping out is not where it's at.
You need to find what you're after.
If you talk to the Man in the sky,
He'll help you get it all together.
You can tune in to His wavelength, if you try.
You need not sit on the floor and meditate
just to reach a high mental state.
Some say "tune in to the universal consciousness."
I say, be conscious of truth that's vital to all of us.
So many don't know where life is leading to.
But what's the trip when life is through?
Where will you spend <u>your</u> eternity?
Turn on to the promise of Heaven!
Turn off to the New Age philosophy,
and come into the spiritual dimension.
You'll enter a whole new reality.
If you think it's going to be a drag, you're wrong.
You'll turn on to the joy of worship in dance and song!

Emptiness

Many people feel but seldom say
that something's missing in life today.
Many people are merely existing,
and they are not really living.
They won't find happiness the way they think they will.
Down deep inside they hurt, and feel empty still.
That's part of what <u>your</u> life's all about.
But this is not how you wanted life to turn out.
And something is seriously wrong,
because all of your hopes are gone.
It's an empty feeling living without
the God who so often helps us out.
Of course, you could lift yourself up in society,
but without God in your life, it would be empty -
empty through all the years that are before you.
Do you know what the Lord can do for you?
There's no broken dream He can't fulfill.
There's no empty soul He can't fill.
Just come to Him humbly with an open hand.
God's supply exceeds the demand.
What would you like to ask God for?
Something you can keep for evermore?

Ask Him.
Call on Him now.

Someone Loves You

All is dark at the end of the day
as you walk along a solitary pathway.

And in the shadows, tears fall.
Who sees and wants to help you through it all?

Who upholds your little world,
and keeps it from falling apart?
Who makes the light of hope
shine forever in your heart?

You would not feel unimportant to Him
if you would consider
that however vast the heavens are,
His love for you is bigger.

Do you know that someone loves you like this?
Should you pretend He does not even exist?

My Turn To Talk

You might get up and leave
before you hear me through.
You might not even believe
that God's love is for you.
Dear, He loves you! The devil can't change that.
But he has you fooled, scared, and blind as a bat!
The devil tattles to God about how you have misbehaved.
So do something that will really freak him out: Get saved!
Christ wants to save you because
He cares about you. Yes he does!
Am I hearing you right? Are you saying
you don't believe in that sort of thing?
A Savior wants to rescue you from the pit,
and you tell me you don't want to hear it?
That's dumb! Before I finish my little chat,
I think you'll change your ideas on that!
Wouldn't a God who is loving and good
want what's best for you? Of course He would!
If I ask you to accept Him, would you hiss
or whisper: How can I get out of this?
Well, you don't want this, and you don't want that!
You're so confused and scared, you just want to scat!
Listen, make it easier on yourself and me as well.
Get right with God, and get saved from Hell!
Is that something you just don't want to deal with?
If I tell you about Heaven, would you say that's a myth?
He's prepared heavenly treasure which awaits you.
Now dear, do you still think God hates you?
Though you may feel He's left you out on a limb,
God believes in you. Do you believe in Him?

I Will Help You

Dear, your spiritual life is really going downhill.
If no one else cares enough to help you, I will.
I want to help you, although I
realize you don't even know why.
I want to lead you back to God.
Who is to say that I could not?
I feel God's very own love for you,
but you do not see it as such.
You read this, then you wonder why
I care about you so much.
Try to see your life as an irreplaceable work of art.
Would you let it be walked on 'til it falls apart?
Look at your life – what you've done;
what you've got yourself into –
and consider how far you have fallen
beneath what God wanted for you.
You have let go of every tie to His way,
and helplessly you are drifting away.
You're being swept out to sea without a boat.
In the waves of fear, you wouldn't stay afloat.
I don't want to see you going down.
You'd better head for solid ground.
May I tell you the way to that golden shore?
If you go under, may I lift you up and carry you ashore?

Note To a Young Person

No matter what path in life you pursue,
God is concerned and cares about you.
He loves you so much that He wants to
deliver you from what's tormenting you;
and He wants you to have real happiness.
But you can't be happy, unless
you ask and get His forgiveness.
He wants to see the joy in your eyes,
and to give you a home in Paradise,
all because of perfect love on His part.
He holds a special place for you in His heart.
To you, His hand of love is stretched out still.
And if you ask Him to make you His, He really will.
It's time you and Got get together.
You need Him now more than ever.

Why Do I Need God?

A man came to my house the other day.
I told him about God and he began to say:

"How dare you tell me how to believe! I may drink a few beers,
but I'm successful and well respected among my peers.
I'm a good and honest man, and I even give to charity.
Why do I need God when I've got financial prosperity?"

I should have said that you can't reach Heaven by good works alone.
You've got to repent to get saved from the fire and brimstone.
You may also ask: "Why do I need God when I'm doing just fine on my own?"
You think you can do without God in your life,
but can you do without Him in the afterlife?
Wealth can get you what you want any time you want it,
but it can't get you saved from the bottomless pit.
You think you can get anything you want, and yet,
there are some things you really can't get.
Without God, you can't get His forgiveness,
real peace of mind, Heaven and true happiness.

That's why you need God.

A Divine Friend

Consider how much good it would do
to have a god as a friend to turn to.
Wouldn't you like to have a Divine Friend?
He would take you to a palace after you ascend.
Would you feel honored to enter His throne?
Would you like to become one of His very own?
If you fear that He'd be angry at you
for the things you did or didn't do,
then simply ask Him to forgive you.
Do you know that you have an enemy
who wants to hurt you infinitely,
ruin your life, and cast you into a pit?
But there is a Divine Friend who wants to save you from it.
The enemy never fights fair.
He plans to put you in a pit of despair.
He wants to drag you down into the mire,
but a Divine Friend wants to lift you up higher.
He's a king with a glorious kingdom to share.
And if you make Him yours, He would take you there.
Imagine having a king as a friend, a friend who
would stand up for you on Judgment Day and defend you!
He's the one person you need above all else.
He would stand between you and death itself!
This is the kind of friend He wants to be.
You are loved by the greatest hero in history.
Now can you see how wonderful He really is?
If you want such a friend, just tell Him to make you His.
Then you will belong to a god who loves you!

Letter of Compassion

Dear Miss, can you spare a moment
to consider something very important?
I noticed you looking so sad and blue.
Is there anything that I can do?
Perhaps tell you where happiness comes from,
and what you have to do to get some.
You must be wishing happy days would come.
You've got a lot of sorrow to overcome.
Maybe I could help you out.
Let's sit down and talk about
how to have the joy of living.
I'll make you smile; I'll get you laughing.
And then let's talk about the One who
loves you even more than I do.
It's time you and God get together.
You need His help now more than ever.
I saw you crying in the shadows, dear.
Without any love to bring you cheer,
tell me, what on earth will you do,
and what will ever become of you?
No one seems to care. But I do.
I'll take your hand and say a prayer just for you.

Let God Help You

I

Something has taken away your little song,
and something's troubling you. What's wrong?
Get with God and tell Him what's the matter.
Wouldn't God have the answer?
Why not ask Him to help you?
I'm sure He would know what to do.
I'm sure He could help you out.
That's what I want to talk with you about.
Whatever you're going through,
He has the answer for you.
What you can do about it is pray,
and things just might turn out okay.

II.

Those who hate you just laugh and say that's tough.
Others are waiting to see if you're good enough.
But sometimes you just don't care – you just want to give up.
Sometimes life is just too rough.
And when you feel like you don't even want to try,
and you'd rather just lay down and die, let God help you.
When you're drowning in an ocean of despair,
and you find yourself in a living nightmare,
let God help you.
Without hope, life means just nothing,
and you simply can't go on living.
Listen, let God help you get through this,
before you slip off into the abyss.
Let God help you.

III.

Left to yourself, you'd fall apart.
Let God heal your broken heart.
Sure love has left your life, and you feel desolate.
But let God help you get over it.
After your little light has been lit,
why should a heartbreak make you quit?
Why take this all on yourself,
when you really could have God's help?
If you let Him help you get it all together,
then your mood will surely get better.
Before that problem gets too much to bear,
you'd better take it to Him in prayer.
If you don't, things will just get worse.
Must you bring upon yourself a curse?

IV.

God wants to help you, but you keep pushing Him away,
and you can't be happy that way.
Before the sadness of life overtakes you;
and before the weight of the world breaks you,
let God help you.
God wants you to get right with Him, so that He can
heal the hurt and make you happy again.
And yet He wants to do for you so much more.
But you're holding yourself back. What for?
Is it because you are afraid
because you have never made
things right between Him and you?
Well then, that is just what you need to do.
Make things right between Him and you!

What You Need To Do

Life's brief experience will soon be past,
and what have you done for God and for others that will last?
Earth is crumbling beneath our feet, and soon it will be swept away.
And on what will you stand as you face God on Judgment Day?
If you're not saved, no earthly words could express
how you'll feel when you face the outer darkness.
The door to eternity will shut, from which there is no return.
Don't let that happen to you. It's an awful lesson to have to learn.
It would be to your benefit if you would consider
your need of salvation; your need of a Savior.
If you don't cry out to Him, you will never
find the only way home – back to the Father.
The way to avoid being lost forever you need to hear,
even if it would fill you with great fear.
Being lost forever is a fate which you can prevent.
You can change that fate when you sincerely repent.

This is what you need to do.

Dear Lost Soul,

In this dreadful night you're all alone.
While the wind-swept trees of winter moan,
down the lonely corridors of life you go
without a friend who will end your sorrow.
Somehow you've got turned around and lost your way
among the paths of yesterday.
Where will you go? Where are you bound?
Why stay on the road that leads you down?
Dear lost soul, I know you're out there
among the shadows somewhere.
Do you know someone does care?
That someone who truly loves you
wants to rush to your rescue
before you go where parting is final,
and where separation is eternal.
Before you go and slip out into the abyss,
cry out to God for His forgiveness.
You're the lost soul He wants to find.
Let me share with you from the Bible a word so kind:
"Him that cometh unto Me, will I in no wise cast out."
This is something you should talk to Him about.
He doesn't hate you. He loves you dearly.
You'll find out if you speak to Him sincerely.
He wants to save your soul from eternal loss.
That is why He took your place on the cross.
In God there is hope beyond the grave,
and you are the lost soul He died to save.

Stop!

You're on a collision course with the hereafter.
I want to help you avert a disaster.
Your life will go by so fast.
After the wheels of time go rolling past,
Someone wants to be there for you in the end,
and He wants to be your eternal friend.
Today you may appeal to Him for mercy.
Today get saved and begin your journey
down the road that winds across the years.
At the end of the road, the radiance of Heaven appears.
Why, when it's too late, must you learn?
On the road of life, take the right turn,
or else you'll be filled with dread,
and with fear of what lies ahead.
You're on a collision course with the hereafter.
He wants to help you avert a disaster.
Right now stop at life's intersection,
look both ways, and make a decision.
Decide in a moment of silence
as you stare into the distance.
Which way will you go? Which way will you choose?
Why not take God's way? You've got a Hell to lose!

The Road of Life

We all travel the road of life, but very few
really know where their lives will lead to.
Along the road you have taken,
what is your final destination?
Don't proceed till you figure out where you're at.
You're lost and you've got to find the way back.
You should go no farther until you know
which direction in life to go.
Will you take the high road that leads to
Heaven's glories?
Or will you take the road that leads down
to Hades?
When you come to the end of the road of life,
where will you spend the afterlife?
Heaven is the place you should want to go
more than any other place you know.
It really makes a difference when you
have Heaven to look forward to.

Are you going there?

The Path To Heaven

As you walk the path of your life, consider where it will lead.
Someone to show you the right way is what you need.
But if you run to your friends for counsel, they'll
send you off merrily down the wrong trail.
The correct path is far from theirs.
The path to Heaven must be chosen with care.
Only one path will lead you there.
You should follow the leader whose way is best –
the One who leads us to the Islands of the Blest.
If you follow Him who leads people there,
someday you'll arrive in that land so fair.
Those who are not going with us
will have to face the outer darkness.
After this life, you'll have all eternity before you.
But without God, it holds nothing for you.
Dear, what will happen to you after you die?
Will you go to that heavenly realm on high?
Will you face eternity with God's hand in yours,
taking you to those heavenly shores?
So many will not be allowed to enter.
You don't want to be lost forever.
As someone who cares, I would like to say:
Repent right now and take the right way.
At the crossroads of life, so many take the wrong turn.
I hope you don't. It's an awful lesson to have to learn.

The Spiritual Element

It would be an honor and a delight
to speak to you about the Lord of my life.
It is the Lord who holds the power
that makes a seed grow into a flower,
and causes the circle of life to turn.
The secrets of the Universe man could learn
in a new and wonderful light,
allowing the spiritual element in life.

What you miss is the very truth you need to accept.
It appears that some of your views on this subject
are based on bias and needs to be altered.
Beliefs you've rejected, now should be considered
in a new and wonderful light,
allowing the spiritual element in life.

For your beliefs you have offered no logical reasons;
and some of your strongest held notions
have been shown to be for naught.
Your entire belief system needs to be re-thought
in a new and wonderful light,
allowing the spiritual element in life.

Come to find out, many of man's basic premises are flawed.
The theory of evolution has been proven to be a fraud.
False ideas once cherished are now as nothing.
I'm afraid your entire belief system needs adjusting.

What You Get When You Join God's Kingdom

Throughout recorded history,
there were kings who ruled over humanity
with hate, force, and brutality.
Perhaps you are not aware of
a king whose power over people is love.
He calls Himself a shepherd;
and to be a follower of His,
you put yourself under the rule
of the greatest king there is!
If you want to enter His kingdom,
you must repent and be forgiven.
And if you decide against doing evil things,
you'll be placed under the dominion of the King of Kings!
You get to have Him rule in your life,
instead of the enemy.
You get to be reconciled with God,
instead of feeling guilty.
Then you will have peace of mind
in place of your fears.
You get to reign with Him
for a thousand years!
Besides, you get to personally know
this King of Heaven who loves you so!
You get to form a friendship with the King of Glory!
Then you can tell others His Divine love story.
And it doesn't stop there: It only gets better!
You get to have life's greatest treasure!
The joy of a spiritual rebirth!
On top of that, you'll get something of highest worth:
real meaning to your life, and purpose!
You'd have to be out of your mind to reject this!
You get to have the greatest thing:
A complete pardon from Heaven's King.
You get to be adopted by the Heavenly Father,
to be His dear son, or His dear daughter.
You get to have His love beyond measure.

Then in Heaven, you get to live forever.
Now you can't beat that for a deal, can you?
These are things of eternal value.
Nothing material can even begin to compare
with the sum of God's gifts; and it doesn't stop there!
You get to return to Paradise someday;
and to have a beautiful home in a kingdom far away.

To a Student

In school, you are taught to think in conformity
to an agenda which excludes or opposes Christianity.
But what if Christianity were real instead of fake?
Then wouldn't you be making a big mistake
to base your entire life upon a lie?
To think there's no Hell or Heaven after you die?
Now you are torn between two eternities.
You've been taught they are both fantasies.
And since you're a victim of mind-conditioning,
you need to get what's wrong out of your thinking.
You need to separate truth from falsehood.
It would be to your advantage if you would.
Think deeper until you find the truth amid the deception,
and then you'll wonder why you've never made the connection.

Divine Truth

What I want to talk to you about
is why Divine Truth should not be kept out.
That cuts you out of all that you would gain.
Everyone who believes in truth is on my thought plane.
Divine Truth is most always met with rejection.
This is partly due to humanistic lies and deception.
You've been lied to, and you've been cheated out
of the most important truth that you could learn about.
On your behalf, here's what God wants me to say:
There are those who are leading you the wrong way.
They have no moral compass, yet they tell you what to do.
They speak of truth as it appears from their narrow view.
They speak of the positive as if it's bad news,
and they speak of the negative as if it's the thing to choose.
They put it to you wrong, and I'm trying to put it to you right.
Amid all the confusion, I'm here to shed a little light.
Their humanistic belief system is too narrow, and too small.
Why not acquire spiritual truth which is vital to us all?
Why not get saved? Get with the only One
who can give you eternal life in Heaven.
You may think Heaven is just a mere fantasy,
but it's a place which exists in another reality.
The land where life begins anew is a vision of splendor.
And in this land of joy, you could live forever.
This wonderful truth should not be kept out.
It is something to really get excited about.
And right now you have a chance to discover
how you could live in that land forever.
He wants to be your Savior, so make Him yours.
Then you will be destined to those happy shores.

Man Is Lost

Man once lived in paradise at one time in history.
Then man fell from his first estate of glory.
And still today, in some deep, profound way,
man longs to return to God someday.
Man is like a child in a forest who decided to wander,
and somehow lost touch with his Divine Father.
Man is lost and will never find the way back on his own.
Unless he cries out to his Father, he will remain lost and alone.
Each lost soul who searches for the way
is like a child trying to reach his Father
and his lost home beyond Earth.
Man's homing instinct causes him to long for
another world – that perfect world where his Father is.
His Father he does not even know.
Over millennia, man's origin has been forgotten,
and the truth of paradise has been lost.
Yet man's brightest hope is to realize
that he can someday return to paradise.

The World Divine

The hope in man of someday reaching paradise will always persist.
Somewhere out there a perfect world does exist.
It's a place which people dream of going to
after their lives on Earth are through.
Now perhaps it's drawing you,
and you want to find the way to
the World Divine. Like a star,
it was always too far
from you. But right today,
I'll show you the way.
Oh imagine! You could spend eternity
in a world of perfection and beauty!
You're not just imagining it,
this place really does exist!
It's a land of perfect beauty
where you could spend your eternity;
where the tree of life is growing,
and the River of Life is flowing.
Think how beautiful this pace must be!
But most people will never see
the World Divine.
Those who see it are filled with wonder and awe
to see a world devoid of human flaw.
Imagine! A perfect world to live in!
So few people seem to believe in
the World Divine. And so few are even aware
that they could spend eternity there.
One must accept Christ, and if you do,
then after life on Earth is through,
you'll enter that land where dreams come true!
The World Divine! And once you enter,
you'll want to stay there forever.
You will gladly leave the things of Earth behind,
because you will have better things in mind.
You'll have eternal youth, joy supernal,
an immortal body and life eternal!

In the World Divine, there are forests, birds, and flowers, too.
And there are lots of exciting things to do.
If you repent and decide to go God's way,
this is where you're going to live someday.

Poems About Heaven

A Higher World

There's a world far more beautiful than Earth,
where God rules over all, and love is of greatest worth.
Our heavenly home where we'll never die
is in that land out there beyond the sky.
On a planet which does not rotate or revolve,
the age-old riddle of time has been solved.
We are here for but a moment in eternity.
After this life, a higher world is our destiny.
We are destined to a higher world out in space.
Someday we will leave this world without a trace,
and be taken in the twinkling of an eye
to that heavenly kingdom beyond the sky.
Across the darkness we'll sail away
to the land of eternal day.
With joy and excitement we'll enter
that land where all is at peace forever.
Once there, in the presence of God's light,
we'll see everything beautiful in life.
Right now, everything looks dark and hopeless.
I know that, but always remember this:
That in some joyful new day
on a fairer world far away,
life will be so much better.

Home For All Eternity

I

As you look up at the stars some lonely night, remember,
this world is not our home forever.
We'll leave it all behind for something better.
Somewhere out there in the galactic sea,
there's an island of beauty
which will be our home for all eternity.

II

It seems like an unreachable distance
across the great celestial expanse.
But there's no distance too great for God to cross,
and there's no gulf of darkness He can't carry us across.
He who placed the Earth in orbit
will someday lift us out of it.
We'll lift off the surface of this planet,
and head out into the vastness of the infinite.
We'll journey across the starry skies
to that land where no one ever dies.
And on that island of beauty,
we'll have a home for all eternity.

III

We know we'll be there someday,
although it seems like an unreachable distance away.
This is the blessed hope of the believer.
For most of us who speak of the rapture,
we speak of being lifted away.
We'll leave this planet on some exciting future day,
and sail across the ocean of space
to escape the tribulation of the human race.
Many will be left here alone
after the Father takes us home.
For us the first day in eternity will dawn.
We need a home after life on Earth is gone.
Somewhere out there in the galactic sea,
there's an island of beauty
which will be our home for all eternity.

We'll Sail Away

We'll leave this planet someday
for that fairer world far away.
This is what our whole lives have been leading up to.
Think deeper and you'll know this is true.
When the last trumpet will blow,
God will call us out of the land of the shadow
to take us to our homeland far away.
We'll leave this world on that day,
and set sail out upon the galactic sea,
and disappear into infinity.
We'll sail away, we'll sail away.
And though the ocean of space is wide,
we'll sail across it to the other side.
We'll sail through the galactic sea,
'til we reach that island of beauty
which we were always longing for.
When we reach that distant shore,
then we'll become citizens of a loftier clime,
and walk on the shores where the timeless meet with time.

Return To Paradise

To return to paradise:
This is our high destiny!
At the end of the earthly journey,
we'll be lifted off the surface of this planet,
and launch out into the vastness of the infinite.
Life beyond Earth:
This is what more and more intrigues us!
We'll leave this planet someday on a grand exodus,
and return to paradise!
This is our high destiny!
At the end of the earthly journey,
when God calls us out of the land of the shadow –
back to that land which was lost so long ago –
we'll fly across the starry skies
to that realm where no one ever dies.
When it's time for us to leave, we'll be lifted away.
We'll leave this planet on some exciting future day,
to return to paradise!

Paradise

Throughout life, each of us has a path to follow.
It's leading to something greater than we know.
Somewhere out there, a paradise awaits me and you.
That's what our whole lives have been leading up to.
We feel something greater exists beyond the life we know.
Perhaps it's the paradise which man has lost so long ago.
It seems that in some deep, profound way,
the soul of man longs to return to God someday.
Though we must complete our mission to lost humanity,
sometimes we long to leave this world, don't we?
We'll let go of all our earthly ties
and leave for a land of paradise.
No matter how disappointing life gets, remember,
in that land you'll have a life that's so much better.
And you'll see everything differently.
You'll see how beautiful life will be
in some exciting future day
in a kingdom far away.

Our Home On High

We are a long way from home, like a lonely ship at sea.
Amid the vast ocean of space, there's an island of beauty –
an island to which we are destined
when our earthly journey comes to an end.
There's a need for you and me
to have a home for all eternity –
a home awaiting us at the end of the earthly journey.
We think of our homeland, as we lift up our eyes:
that homeland to which our hearts have stronger ties.
Someday we'll have to say goodbye.
We must return to our home in the sky.
We long to reach that distant homeland where God is.
Across the stars, God's kingdom extends. It links our hearts with His.
Never lose your connection with God.
That is your only link to the world beyond.

The World Beyond

I

Far, far away…beyond all hurt, heartbreak, and strife;
and beyond all the disappointments of life,
There's a kingdom where only good is allowed to enter;
and where things of beauty are forever.
This kingdom exists in a world beyond the one we see.
It's thought to have only symbolic reality,
and to exist only in a fairy tale.
Compared to it, Earth with all its riches would pale.

II

None of the cares of Earth will matter
on the glad day that you enter…the World Beyond.
Only eternal things will matter when everything fades from view.
Then this world with all its allure, will lose its hold over you.
It's not the end when life is through.
You step off this world into…the World Beyond.
When you pass from this life to another,
you'll have a whole new realm to discover.
Then you'll be filled with the most beautiful peace,
and the glory of your new life will never cease.
Here you will have the joy of the life divine,
which so many have sought in vain to find.
So many are called, but so few will respond
and join us in the World Beyond.

III

Here is the greatest beauty of the Creator's art,
and it was fashioned for us out of the love of His heart.
When it's time for you to enjoy those eternal delights,
God will call you from across the starry heights.
His words will come down to you from somewhere above,
spoken with perfect beauty and perfect love.
The kindest words you will every hear are His,
They'll fill your mind with all that glory is.
The most welcome words you'll ever hear
is the Lord saying, "You'll spend eternity here."

IV

After the angels open for you the everlasting doors,
some things so glorious will be yours;
such as an immortal body, eternal youthfulness,
a perfect mind, everlasting happiness,
a vast inheritance all your own,
and some presents given to you by the King on His throne.
Through palatial halls, angels will escort you along.
Then you'll hear notes of a most lovely song,
charming you as you listen.
Its beauty is beyond description.
Angels will lead you to a home built just for you.
You'll look out a window and see all things new.
The realization you just can't get over
is to know this is home, and this is forever!

V

Outside, you'll see idyllic scenes of nature in abundance.
From a hill, you'll see a city off in the distance
with spires and domes made of jewels that gleam.
At first you might think this is all a dream.
Just wait, and when it comes your turn,
you may be surprised to learn
that all of this really is true!
The Lord has prepared a place for you.
This is a place too beautiful to imagine.
This is where your new life will begin!

Government
Corruption

Religious Discrimination

My fellow Americans, it's great to be with you today.
And I'm honored that you want to hear what I have to say.
You are strong enough to face the truth which I speak.
Leftist liberals can't, because they are cowards, and they are weak.

Leftist liberals have declared war against the Christian religion.
This is their dirty little secret, and they want it kept hidden.
They are filibustering and discriminating against Christians
who have been selected for top-flight government positions.

Leftist liberals are bigoted and intolerant of Christianity;
and they want all mention of God removed from society.
To do this would be a free speech violation,
and would constitute religious discrimination.

In many of our public schools today,
they have deprived students the right to pray;
to sing carols, and to even celebrate Christmas.
If a student even mentions the word Jesus,

in an oral book report and not in a swearing way –
that student will get an F or an E for the day.
This is wrong. This is a blatant social injustice,
which has been illegally imposed upon us.

People, I bring this to your attention, that you may
wake up to what's really happening in our country today,
and motivate our leaders to do something about it.
Let's end religious discrimination! We're better off without it!

When there is legal grounds to sue, call the A.C.L.J.
Let's deal with this problem in the appropriate way,
without resorting to violence, which would be a mistake.
There's one other recourse of action for us to take.

Just don't vote for leftist liberals on election day!
Because they are taking our rights and freedoms away!
Come on, people, stand up, raise your fists and shout:
Vote them out! Vote them out! Vote them out! Vote them out!

Our Rights

Our system of democracy is eroding more each day,
because our rights and freedoms are being taken away.
If nothing is done to stem the tide,
a lot more of our rights will be denied.
Our rights and freedoms are being uprooted one by one,
and we demand to know what is going to be done!
To ensure that our rights will be protected,
a viable solution must be implemented.
The worst problems in our government can and must be solved,
or eventually our system of democracy will be dissolved.
We've got to stem the tide before it's too late!
We've got to take strong steps to set things straight,
or else our most cherished freedoms will be wiped out.
Our future as a free nation is in serious doubt.
We are seeing our nation being torn apart
by leftist liberals who are traitors at heart.
With one inroad after another, they are getting stronger.
I say, let's not allow this to go on any longer!
Enough is enough! Now's the time to take a stand,
and make our voices heard throughout the land!

The Law and Judicial Corruption

If we are to continue to live in a free society,
we must stop the trend toward oligarchy.
We are becoming a nation ruled by judges,
and our justice system is starting to fall to pieces.
But if strong action is taken,
we could correct the situation
before it gets too far out of hand.
Someone's got to ask the leaders of our land
why the law isn't being enforced against judicial corruption,
and against evidence planted by corrupt policemen.
A lot of this would stop if they were arrested.
This is one solution which must be implemented
so that the problem may be corrected.
But many of our leaders don't have the will to fight
against these wrongs in order to make things right.
Some judges break the law to suit some liberal purpose,
and they change the law without due process.
Is this how the law is supposed to run?
No! The appropriate steps must be taken!
To do nothing is downright irresponsible!
Those who break the law must be held accountable.
Why isn't the law being enforced against left wing senators?
If all the truth were known, some of them would be considered traitors!
Some of our leaders who belong to anti-American organizations,
continue to commit crimes against the soul of our nation,
because the law is no longer enforced against them.
We've got to do something to correct this problem.
To do nothing is downright irresponsible!
Those who break the law must be held accountable!
Why doesn't anyone put them under arrest?
This is an outrage! And that's why we protest!
My fellow Americans, let's not stand for this!
We demand justice! We demand justice! We demand justice!
Strong action must be taken
in order to correct the situation.
This really needs to be done to ensure
that our system of democracy will endure.

The Enemy From Within

The good people of this country need to be alerted
that our system of democracy is being subverted.
Some of our rights and freedoms are being taken away
by people in power who oppose the American way.
It is our system of democracy that they are subverting.
What we see happening to our country is very disconcerting.
Our government officials have got to awake,
as the future of our nation is clearly at stake.
Swift and decisive action must be taken
to stop the work of the enemy from within.
Leftist liberals are making inroads more and more each day.
They have threatened civil war if they can't have their own way.
It makes you wonder if our country has already been
secretly taken over by some enemy from within.
Into all branches of government they have infiltrated.
Their cause is more sinister than at first anticipated.
Full disclosure of this matter should be made known.
If bias and partiality have not been shown,
why isn't the law being enforced, then
against left wing senators and congressmen?
I say, let's do away with this double standard!
Let's protest and make our position heard!
Whatever we're up against, it must be faced!
This blight on our society must be erased!

Evolution
Vs. Creationism

The Lies of Evolution

Students of today are forced to learn evolution,
even though it has been totally disproven.
It's not an established fact, and I'll tell you why.
Evolution is an established lie!
In secular schools, why aren't students
allowed to bring forth proof or evidence
to show that evolution – no matter how it flies –
is <u>not</u> based on science, but based on lies?
Teaching lies in school should be an unlawful act.
Evolution is merely a theory taught as fact.
They say that man came from apes, and therefore,
we have no souls.
But the Darwin theory is shot full of holes!
They say that we have evolved into what we are today,
and that we were not created the Biblical way.
Officially, life came from nowhere. Isn't that odd?
But really, creation came from the hand of God.
What we were taught about human origin is just a lie!
I'll believe in evolution when pigs can fly!

Two Examples of Prehistoric Man:

1. "Lazaretto Man" – Body found intact, preserved by being frozen in ice on a mountain. Made international news. Funny thing, he has no resemblance to an ape.

2. "Vladimir Man" – A caveman with no ape-like features. He wears a shirt and trousers – much to the horror of evolutionists! What's even more amazing is that he wears mechanical gadgets! So much for the evolution theory!

Two False Examples of Prehistoric Man:

1. "Neanderthal Man" – Fraud! Not part ape. Proven to be totally human.

2. "Piltdown Man" – Fraud! Faked fossils exposed by Popular Science Monthly and Readers Digest in 1956. Schools, however, ignored this.

A Superior Intelligence

There seems to be a purpose and an intelligence
behind everything in existence.
Intelligence even behind the force
which moves every electron,
and keeps every world in its course –
stabilized in a perfect balance
between gravity and centrifugal force.
With order and precision, the Universe was designed.
Creation didn't come about by coincidence. It took a mind.
Laws of physics were used which are known,
as well as other laws which are as yet unknown.
The ordered design of the solar system
appears just like the design of every atom.
Electrons revolving around the nucleus are
much like the planets revolving around a star.
With such order in creation,
there must be an intelligence behind it.
With precision, each star system
is put together as if someone designed it.
I conclude that there is a Superior Intelligence
which orders everything in existence.

Superior Beings

Life Among the Heavens

I want to address something about
which many people wonder.
It is the possible existence of any other
intelligent life among the heavens.
Did God create beings who have
formed superior civilizations?
There really could be such beings
among the heavens somewhere.
How can they say there is none,
without even going there?
Even if they had discovered
life on Mars and Venus,
it would be classified
top secret, and kept from us.
Alien life? The heathen don't want to hear it!
To them it's a foolish dream,
simply because it does not fit
into their narrow thought scheme.
I'd love to share what I know,
but I must take into consideration
whether or not they are sufficiently level-headed
to handle the information.
They think there is no other life
in all the constellations.
Since they wouldn't believe what I'd say,
they'll have to do without the information.
I could lay it out for them with simple logic
to make sure they would understand,
but I will not lay the secrets of the Universe
in the palm of their hand.

What's Out There?

Is there other life in the heavens somewhere?
Many people wonder what's really out there.
A flying disc is seen, and no one tells us what it is.
And no matter what explanation the Air Force gives,
man is still puzzled by the great unknown.
He can't know what's out there by theories alone.
It requires an unbiased and thorough evaluation
in order to determine the truth and its implications.
What's out there in the great celestial expanse
is beyond all man's knowledge and experience.
As man looks at all the celestial wonders,
he has more questions and less answers.
People ask: Is there intelligent life in outer space?
I say to the entire human race:
Yes. There is God, the angels, the Watchers,
the Cherubim, the Seraphim, and many others.
Magnificent things exist beyond the little world we know,
and surely the Father has made it so.

It's Possible

You may wonder what's out there among the stars.
Do other civilizations exist which are superior to ours?
It's possible there's an advanced alien race
which exists somewhere in outer space.
If alien visitors come here, it's possible
that their purposes are peaceful.
The ships which the astronauts saw have no earthly affiliation.
They may be stationed up there to protect Earth from invasion.
Do not discard this without first considering
that some things are beyond your understanding.
Can you know the truth of this matter without
even making an effort to find out?
It requires an unbiased and thorough evaluation
in order to determine the truth and its implications.
The possibility of beings who are superior to us
provides us with a fascinating subject to discuss.
It's possible that many different aliens
come here from other worlds in the heavens.
Technologically, they would be superior to mortals.
It's possible that some of these aliens are actually angels.
And it's possible that a people from a loftier clime
travel to Earth beyond the barrier of time!
We will not throw all that is fantastic
into the realm of the unreal,
if we have the faith of a child who believes
that something so amazing could be real.

Supernatural Beings

Many beings carry out missions on Earth
in their service to the King of the Universe.
The Cherubim and Seraphim actually are real.
And since they aren't from Earth, they are extraterrestrial.
And although it may be above top secret,
some keep an ongoing patrol of this planet,
according to Zechariah, chapter one,
verse ten in the Revised Standard Version.
Some angels are guardians who provide protection.
And some are mighty angelic warriors
who fight against principalities and powers.
Demons try to destroy the lives of believers,
and often claim the souls of unbelievers.
They'd easily claim the souls of all mortals,
were it not for the help of Christ and His angels.
Whatever He wants done is brought about
by legions of angels who carry it out.
On their base of operations, they continually plan
how to counter the forces which fight against man.
There are two opposing forces in the solar system,
yet man cannot separate himself from them.
There are the forces of light, and the forces of darkness.
For you who choose the light, God gives His promise
that the forces of darkness will not hurt you.
While you are under His shield, they will not be allowed to.
Wherever you go, and whatever you do,
there are forces of light protecting you.
So you can feel safe and secure under His fatherly eye.
To Him you're a dear little child who can't understand why
you are being watched by a superior intelligence.
God is carefully keeping your little world under surveillance.

A Report on Angels

Some people believe only what they can see.
They think angels have no reality.
To accept the possibility of actual angels
inspires us to think on higher levels.
Have you ever been helped by a total stranger
who mysteriously vanished around a corner?
Maybe that was an angel.
Angels can vanish or appear merely at will.
They have control over all natural forces,
and have power over matter as well.

Angels have unthinkable power,
and knowledge of the highest order.
In many ways they are superior to earthlings.
They are not controlled by human feelings.
Angels – unlike evil spirits or demons –
care not to converse with humans.
Evil spirits and demons fight against man
by whatever means and ways they can.
They try to make mortals become evil.
They love to destroy the souls of people
by turning them away from God and what is right.
But when God sends the forces of light,
then the forces of darkness do not stay.
They move off into the distance far away.

Angels are a form of alien life
with a God-oriented society;
and they are under His orders
to keep vigil over His human colony.
They are not allowed to use force,
or to alter history's present course.
They who serve in such a high cause
must also obey the universal laws,
by the decree of the Watchers from upon high.
So spoke the prophet, and so must I.

What Are the Cherubim?

What are Cherubim? Those from a loftier clime
who travel in ships beyond the barrier of time?
This advanced race of people actually are aliens
who carry out God's orders among other civilizations.
Their interstellar ships fly without wings;
and with them, they do the strangest things,
such as vanish off radar screens,
or make right angle turns at high speeds.
If you ask the Air Force if these ships are real, they will lie.
They will say it's a weather balloon, or a trick of the eye.
If you ask me, I'd refer you to God's Word in Ezekiel.
You'll find they are under God's command, and they are real.
When you read how the Cherubim transported the prophet,
it's so astonishing you might have trouble believing it.
Should the "living creatures" Ezekiel rode with
be relegated to the realm of legend and myth?
In school, we were taught that the Cherubim are mythological.
Since they have sky ships, they may be super-technological.
We know they are superior to man, but it's quite another thing
to know that they serve and obey Christ as their King.
The concept of higher life forms in the galaxy
is a truth which is popularly regarded as fantasy.
But the thought of them carrying out missions for Heaven's King
presents a more serious threat to the pagan way of thinking.
Suddenly they have a whole new problem to deal with,
so they go into denial and say it's nothing but a myth.
Did you know that angels and Cherubim actually are real?
And since they aren't from Earth, they are extraterrestrial.
If they keep an ongoing patrol of this planet,
that information would be above top secret.

Ancient Gods

God-like visitors from outer space
are found in the legends of every race.
Alien beings who visited Earth throughout history
could have been the so-called gods of mythology.

Perhaps the most amazing fact in world history
is that there were two gods who were not consigned to mythology.
Quetzalcoatl and Kukulkhan were actual beings
who came to South America and became kings.

Quetzalcoatl civilized the Aztecs, and Kukulkhan, the Mayans.
Both of them abolished human sacrifice and the worship of demons.
And they both taught their people an advanced culture,
and to worship the one true God, who is the Creator.

We today consider them gods for their super-human accomplishments,
and for their super-human knowledge in many branches of science.
Their accomplishments and knowledge were super-human not for today,
but for back then, which was 7,000 years ago, historians say.

They are the only gods who are not considered mythological.
It's amazing that they are officially recognized to be historical.
What's even more amazing is that the Ancient Aztecs and Mayans
claimed that these beings came to Earth from the heavens!

They did not consider these kings to be of the human race.
They seem to have imported culture from another world in space.

Prophecy

Interstellar Flight

Today we face the most monumental challenge in history:
to build ships fit to sail through the vastness of infinity.
Our faith needs to be broadened to embrace
this bold new challenge of outer space.
Travel to the stars: this is our high destiny!
This daring quest will someday become a reality!
Earthman now living will stand on Mars,
and bridge the gulf between the stars.
We have the heavens yet to explore.
Man's achievements in the field of space travel are no more
than the first footsteps of a child, compared to those of the Cherubim.
A clue to the secret of their propulsion system
may be a wheel in the middle of a wheel.
This clue was given to us by Ezekiel.
There are clues throughout the Bible, and we need to study each of these.
To a higher life form, man may represent a disease
which must not be allowed to spread to other worlds in space.
Man would soon corrupt a virgin world which never fell from grace.
Is, then, the challenge of interstellar flight only a faded dream?
Will man ever reach the stars? Impossible, it would seem.
Yet perhaps this and every daring quest
will be realized during the thousand year reign of Christ.
Until then, perhaps unregenerate Man is too corruptible
to be entrusted with the secrets which make interstellar flight possible –
secrets, such as gravity control, time neutrality,
inertial deflection, gravitic propulsion, and free energy.
These things would improve our lives to a great degree,
and would have a great impact on our technology.
When these inventions will have wide acceptance and distribution,
they'll bring mankind into a space age revolution.
It's astonishing what God has in store for us!
The greatest challenges are yet before us!
The greatest mysteries are yet to unravel,
such as how to use gravity for space travel.
Perhaps man will one day cross the galactic ocean
in ships powered by gravity and perpetual motion.

The prophet Obadiah implies that we will someday make our nest in the stars.
We should not derogate someone whose ideas differ from ours.
We should, rather, set aside our ego sufficiently
enough to question those ideas intelligently,
that we may learn new information
through a clear-headed and unbiased evaluation.
When we learn the original meaning of cherub was flying machine,
then suddenly we know what certain Bible passages mean,
such as the strange passage which Samuel wrote:
I quote: He rode upon a cherub and did fly, unquote.
It's so fascinating to learn in Ezekiel, chapter three,
how the Cherubim flew the prophet to a distant city.
The secrets of advanced Cherubim technology
presents a most challenging subject of study.
In a classroom of the Cosmos, we could learn great lessons,
such as the meaning of the signs and wonders in the heavens,
which the Son of God Himself referred to;
or the meaning of the prehistoric airport in Nasca, Peru;
or the flying object in Zechariah 5:11 and 5:2,
which sat upon her own base;
or the Watchers in the Book of Daniel who came from outer space!
To learn a fantastic revelation requires the faith of a child, who
believes that something so amazing could be true.
We need to approach the unexplained not as the heathen do,
and not as those who deny God's Word,
but as children who believe there is still mystery and wonder left in the world.
Earth has been our cradle;
the Solar System is our kindergarten;
the Universe will be our university.
There's so much to learn, and so exciting it will be
when we, too, will sail out into infinity.

Free Energy

An invention is soon to be designed
which will provide free energy to all mankind.
It will harness the power of gravity
as an unlimited source of free energy!
This power can be tapped into anywhere
and it exists in abundance everywhere.
People will start using the power of gravity,
because it will provide free energy.
Free energy for every building where power is needed!
Free energy to replace natural gas for every home that is heated!
That will mean no more utility bills to pay!
We will tear off our meter boxes and throw them away!
Just imagine! Free energy will be ours
to power our homes, buildings and cars!
Gasoline companies won't be able to compete.
The use of gasoline will become obsolete.
Other applications for this invention
are too far beyond belief to mention.
Free energy and gravity control
would greatly benefit the world as a whole,
because the power of gravity is free.
Oh what a blessing to humanity!

Cars of the Future

I have wonderful news for everyone!
The gasoline engine will be replaced by a superior one –
one that doesn't cost anything to run,
because it will use a fuel we won't have to pay for!
We won't have the fear of running out of gas anymore.
Cars will never be on empty
if they run on free energy;
and they will never have a dead battery.
But it will really make you surprised
when all the weight of your car is neutralized
by a push of a button to the anti-gravity device.
In the future, wouldn't it be nice
to drive in the air when the roads have ice?
And you won't crash up when your brakes fail.
Just press a button, and up in the air you'll sail!

Right now, all of this seems like fantasy.
But someday all of this will become a reality.

End Time Events

In the heavens, signs and wonders portend
a catastrophe at the time of the end.
A day of doom will befall human civilization,
followed by the horrors of a great tribulation.
Much of the world has been forewarned.
And still the truth they need to hear is scorned.
But all that the Bible predicts will come to pass,
just as it always did in the past.
These people need to know that God could save them,
and help them escape the coming world cataclysm.
God has a plan. To save people from being destroyed,
a divine rescue squad is poised, and ready to be deployed.
Those who have accepted salvation will be taken into space
to avoid the suffering which shall befall the human race.
After the Father takes us home across the galaxy,
many will be left here to face the global catastrophe.
Mankind faces a nuclear holocaust during the tribulation;
and a fireball will strike the planet, causing major devastation.
If a comet hurls down and hits the sea,
would it not flood every country?
This could wipe out all human life. Can you imagine
what's holding back the Father's hand? It's compassion.

The Time of the End

Amid the vast ocean of space, Earth is an island
where the enemy of the Lord makes his last stand.
To the Seraphim, it's a world of rebellion,
where the fallen angels were cast from Heaven.
To the advanced Cherubim, it's a backward planet,
and they have no desire to live in it.
To the Watchers approaching our solar system,
Earth is where their assignment takes them.
To God, who sees in a larger sense,
Earth is a colony under Fatherly guidance.
From Eden, eons ago,
He planted it, and made it grow.
At first there was a paradise and two people.
In comes the enemy. Earth is now filled with evil.
But this is not how God wanted it
in the beginning when He planted it.
He's going to have to let it go and start all over again;
and this time His Son will rule instead of man.
'Til then, we'll see if humanism works, and if it suffices.
When man is left alone to himself and his own devices,
he will bring upon himself worldwide suffering and tribulation.
It's painful for God to allow the fall of civilization.
Very few people can comprehend
that this is the time of the end.
Planets are tossed among the stars like milky dust,
but they, too, have their time.
Your days, and even the stars are all numbered.
You can straighten out the difficulties in your little world,
but you don't have much time, do you?
Life on Earth is temporal, and we are all just passing through.
Your journey through life: Where will it take you?
When you hear the last whistle blow,
you'll have to leave; but where will you go?
Some souls arrive in the land of happiness,
and some arrive in the gulf of darkness,
where there is no salvation.

But all people are in the process of leaving for a destination.
We may deduce from a sacred text
that Earth is a way station between one life and the next.
There are the passengers who are waiting for
the day they reach that distant shore.
They will be taken to a land far away,
and their arrival there will be their happiest day.
The heavenly gates will open and they will enter.
This life is not all you've got: There is the afterlife, which is forever.

Doomsday

We have entered the final phase of human history.
Most will not survive the coming world calamity.
In the Holy Scriptures, the prophets have shown
how civilization will end in fire and brimstone.
God saw how the end was to be.
You can't change the prophecy.
What the Bible predicts will come to pass,
just as it always did in the past.
When we try to tell people how to avoid the grief,
we find that their doubt and disbelief
is too big of a barrier to overcome.
But the fact remains, doomsday will come.
The signs of the times tell us that the end is near.
Those who are saved have no need to fear,
because they will escape the Great Tribulation,
which is described in the Book of Revelation.
A return to God is the last hope for a doomed planet.
And if they will not repent or believe it,
they will have to face the horrors of global war,
worse than the world has ever seen before.
It's all there in God's Word for them to read.
But will they listen? Will they heed?
This message may be mocked, and it may be scorned,
but they can't say that they haven't been warned!

One Thousand Years

There will be a dawn of a new era for man
after Christ comes back to Earth again.
It will be that grand and glorious day as foretold
by the sages and prophets of old
when the King of Heaven appears
to rule the world for one thousand years!
This corrupt world system will be brought to an end.
After the Son of the Highest will descend
on the Mount of Olives, there'll be an earthquake.
Then the powers of darkness will tremble and shake.
Faced with dire warnings; deadlocked with division,
great generals will meet and pause in the Valley of Decision.
Finally, they will decide to move in one accord,
in an all-out assault against the angels of the Lord.
But the forces against Him will face defeat,
and all the nations will be put under His feet one thousand years!
Then He will be greeted everywhere with loud ovation;
and there will be cheers, shouts and screams of jubilation
from the lowest valleys to the highest mountain peaks!
But they stand in awe and silence when He speaks.
It will be so amazing to see that such a man is real
before whom all the world leaders bow and kneel!
In every country His flag will be unfurled,
for He will be the Monarch of the World one thousand years!
All of the governments will be upon His shoulders,
and we His people will carry out His orders
one thousand years!
He will not limit Himself just to ruling and religion.
Every facet of life will be improved under His direction.
A new enthusiasm will take the world by storm,
as every sector of society begins to transform.
A utopian system will be established,
and all human ills will then be abolished.
With great joy our hearts will sing,
and all the Earth will be filled with the glory of the King!
The King will remove the curse

which sin had brought upon the Earth.
Every desert will blossom,
and we will rise above every problem
to live immortal lives with no miseries.
And we will have no worries for one thousand years!
Sickness and suffering will cease,
and the nations will have peace
one thousand years!
Angels will serve with great glory among men.
Oh how exciting to live then!
For science and belief will unite and have new birth;
and the Dream of Ages will reign on Earth
one thousand years!

We'll Rule the World (Rev. 20:6)

At the end of the age of grace for man,
Christ will come back to Earth again
to defend Israel from being conquered and taken.
The world dictator at that time, who is possessed by Satan,
will order the fighting forces of every nation
to come against Christ and His angels
with weapons like bombs and missiles.
In the Valley of Megiddo, these forces will be deployed.
But they will overlook one little fact: Angels can't be destroyed.
Under the direction of the King of Heaven,
the angels will win the battle of Armageddon.
This victory will be followed by a time of great jubilation.
All over the world there will be shouts of joy and celebration.
All of this will happen just like God's Word says it will.
We'll each be cast in a larger role than we ever thought we'd fill.
We'll be kings and priests (Rev. 5:10). And what's more,
we'll be immortals then. That's first Corinthians fifteen fifty-four.
And by the authority that we'll be given,
we'll rule the world with the King of Heaven.
We'll surmount every difficulty with ease,
because we'll have immortal bodies.
For us there will be no more death, pain or tears;
and we'll rule the world with Him for a thousand years!
We're going to be lifted up high and what's more,
no one's going to keep us down anymore,
because we'll be those who are in authority!
We'll be the new ruling class (the aristocracy).
And the wicked will be our underlings.
We'll be in control; we'll run things!
We're going to be in positions of command,
and the wicked will no longer have the upper hand!
They will do all they can to please us
when we rule the world with Jesus.
He will delegate His authority to us,
that He may accomplish His work through us.
He won't do it all by Himself; that's one reason

why He's going to employ everyone.
Work for us will be exciting and fun,
because we'll each be assigned work we love to do.
He will appoint for us grand goals to pursue.
We'll work tirelessly to bring them all about,
while He orchestrates major projects to be carried out,
such as a plan He will give to us, His people
to rid the world of every source of evil!
We'll turn things around like they should be,
and remove all that's wrong in society.
Society will then undergo a transformation.
Human rights and freedom will be restored to every nation;
government corruption, taxes, and warfare will be abolished.
Just within a year, a utopia will be established!
And every golden dream we have will come true!

The Captain of the Hosts of Heaven

Someday we'll get the word that Christ is here.
In the sky over the Mount of Olives He will appear.
With warring angels He will descend
near the city which He comes to defend.

Every force which comes against Him will fall.
He will be victorious over them all.
Then the armies of Earth will lay down their weapons
before the Captain of the Hosts of Heaven!

All the military forces He will defeat.
All nations will be put under His feet,
and then all power on Earth will be given
to the Captain of the Hosts of Heaven!

At last there's peace. After His enemies surrender,
we'll give Him the greatest hero's welcome ever!
Hostilities between nations will cease,
and He will institute a millennium of peace!

Following his ascent to the throne,
we'll see the greatest celebration ever known.
And after His coronation has taken place,
society will be transformed at a rapid pace.

People will be employed in the service of the Lord,
and all the neighboring planets will be explored.
With a high cause, some will carry out missions in outer space,
and we will learn from a people who have never fallen from grace.

On that day, a new enthusiasm will sweep the Earth,
as the planet undergoes renewal and rebirth;
under a kingdom that will never fall,
ruled by the greatest King of them all –

the Captain of the Hosts of Heaven!

The Battle of Armageddon

We're coming to the final events in human history,
when angels fight the forces in Megiddo Valley.
Human history will end in war,
the likes of which we've never seen before.
The Battle of Armageddon has been foretold
thousands of years ago by prophets of old.
This battle will decide human destiny.
The final events in human history
will be an astonishment to many,
as Christ comes back to Earth to set up His throne,
and to defend Jerusalem from being overthrown;
and as thousand of angels come from Heaven
to engage in the Battle of Armageddon.
It will be a short but furious fight
between Christ and the world's military might.
Earth will shake, and walls will rattle
with the sound and fury of the last battle.
Even the strongest fortress will fall
when the King of Heaven conquers all.
After He defeats all the world's armies,
the world dictator will be brought to his knees.
This defeat in Megiddo Valley
will be an astonishment to many.
On top of a mountain, Christ will set up His throne,
and He will be the greatest King the world has ever known.

Under His Reign

I will open for you a view of the future,
to a day when life will be so much better.
You see how dismal life is under the devil's domain.
But under the King of Heaven's reign,
you'll see how beautiful life can be.
In some joyful new day,
things will change completely.
You'll see wonders undreamed of,
and a totally new technology.
Under His reign, people will pursue loftier things
and carry out missions in outer space for the King of Kings.
When I speak of the millennium,
I speak of an exciting future yet to come.
During His thousand year reign,
you'll have a whole new world of joy to gain.
With immortal bodies, we'll have no more pain.
Eternal youth: This too, will be ours
in some exciting future day
when all the sorrows of life will pass away.

Live In Harmony

We must get away from man's abusive power,
and get back to living in harmony with nature,
and follow the laws of the Creator.
Peace on Earth won't come until we
learn to live in perfect harmony.
This means following the laws of nature,
the laws of life, and the laws of the Creator.
We can only live in harmony with our fellow man,
if we live in love and follow God's plan.
Only then will peace on Earth come.
Peace will come at the dawn of the Millennium.
Then we'll get rid of man's abusive power,
and live in harmony with nature,
and follow the laws of the Creator.
On that day, we'll have no more sorrow.
There will be a peaceful world some bright tomorrow.

Nature Poems

Jeanie

(In this poem, nature is personified: A beautiful unspoiled forest
is much like a beautiful unspoiled girl who I name Jeanie)

Many a secret lies hidden beneath the tall timbers
in a valley of green; in a valley of rivers.
With a gust of a whirlwind, I see someone there.
Jeanie of the summer wind stirs the air.
She urges the leaves to play
in a golden moment on a summer day.
Then she rises upon a zephyr, and makes the trees sway.
She brings clouds together, and blows gently over lakes and rivers
to cool us on a hot summer day. She dances on the waters
in a joyful way, as she gathers up vapors.
She moves the clouds away, gliding on a swirl.
She paints the sunset, and all manner of colors unfurl.

Queen of Nature

I have always found nature's queen
in a valley of quiet; in a valley of green,
where all her beauty can be seen.

As the Queen of Nature gives a ballet,
she dances on the water where sunbeams play,
and skips across the river with flashes of sunray.
I go out to this idyllic place to see her,
and to lie down amid her splendor.
She has brought me gentle whispers
of secrets hidden beneath tall timbers.
She has caresses of a cool breeze
and kisses of flowers and colored leaves.

When I first saw the Queen of Nature,
I was caught breathless at the sight of her.
In a valley of rivers; in a valley of green,
I've captured the beauty of nature's queen.

Nature's Beauty

Let's get out into the country
to enjoy some of nature's beauty.
We'll see nature shine in her finest hour
when the sun comes out after a summer shower;
or just as the sun comes shining through
the foggy mists of morning dew.
Across meadows where tall timbers stand,
and where deer bound freely across the land,
nature's beauty is there for you,
spread over a distant view.
From the top of the mountain,
and all across the horizon,
you can see such dazzling sights,
like the summit of mountain heights.
If you don't like the urban sprawl,
and wish to get away from it all,
then drive out into the country
to enjoy some of nature's beauty.

Man Destroys Nature

Today, too many trees are gone, and now stand walls.
The wilderness is slipping away with every tree that falls.
The beauty of nature is irreplaceable.
But the urban sprawl is inescapable.
The forces of destruction, more or less,
have been unleashed upon the wilderness.
One day nature was all aglow,
with fresh water from melting snow,
whereby rivers used to flow,
and trees stood green in the meadow.
What was once an ancient river is no longer there,
just an open-ended path that leads to nowhere.
I drove out in the woods to a meadow,
to reflect on things of long ago.
I found myself on a forgotten path in the forest,
searching for roads which no longer exist.

Spiritual Truth

The Condition of Man

Man is viewed from the heavens as a backward creature,
because of his hostile and destructive nature.
By the looks of all the chaos and destruction we are seeing,
we might say that man is not a rational being.

It seems the whole world is in upheaval.
Just look what is happening to people.
It's all being recorded by Someone
who's watching us from Heaven.

There's one last hope. Back to God we must turn.
Only then will we find peace; only then will we learn
the most important things we should be living for.
Civilization on Earth has a record of violence and war.

To this day nations are still fighting nations,
when they should be conquering the heavens.
They're stuck in their little world, and they can't see
their destiny among the stars for all eternity.

Foolish Mortals

Those stationed high in the heavens tonight
look down to Earth. They can see the plight
of foolish mortals who never
learn the truth until their lives are over.

Foolish mortals living in darkness, never knowing
where in the afterlife they are going.
So many of them are not even aware
of the golden promise of life that is theirs.

When a nation turns from God and becomes
evil, that's when disaster and calamity comes.
History repeats itself so often,
one could almost predict what will happen.

The plight of foolish mortals who never learn
is to the Lord Himself a great concern.
It is easy for Him to see
how beautiful life on Earth could be,

if they would only follow His way.

Man's Way Vs. God's Way

The Most High, with His infinite mind,
has found a way to save mankind.
And yet, most people choose to live without a Savior.
Man has lost his connection with his Creator.
Through every generation, this is his earthly lot.
Most people think man's way is right, but it is not.
A man goes through this entire life living the way that's wrong,
Only to find out in the end that God's way was right all along.
God's way is the only way that works for man,
yet the world has failed to follow His plan.
Who but that humble Man of Galilee
had the highest plan for humanity?
And yet, the world did not accept its only Savior,
nor did they honor the laws of their Creator.
It is sad that these things are all part of man's plight.
But all things that are wrong will someday be made right.

Disbelief

Many people today don't believe in a Creator.
Earth was built by using the knowledge of the laws of nature.
When you look at the intricate order
of the atomic structure,
you know there is a Creator.
Until they have a spiritual awakening,
these facts will remain beneath their level of thinking.
There are many who consider these things, but so few
can understand and believe the Biblical view.

In our mission to lost humanity,
we find disbelief a chasm which we
cannot cross without great difficulty.
Disbelief is a sign of a small mind, which won't receive
any truth which is beyond it to grasp or believe.
Until they become enlightened, they will never
see beyond the delusion they are under.
And until it dawns on them, they will not even know
that their view of life is distorted and narrow.

They think that we're odd people
because of our belief in the spiritual.
We happen to believe in a Creator
who controls the forces behind all things in nature.
If they were not closed-minded,
they would consider the merits of the Biblical view.
Of course they can't allow themselves to do that,
because they might have to
concede that the Bible is true!

The Answer

People need to look to God's Word for the answer
they could not find.
It has great knowledge and wisdom to inspire
the human mind.
God's Word has the answer they are searching for.
They ask: "After we die, does life go on for evermore?"
Some people think they have no hope
to hold on to.
When they come to the end of the rope,
they ask: "What are we to do?"
In tears, lost souls send out signals of despair.
They ask: "Is life's answer among the heavens somewhere?"
This is one of the greatest questions ever asked.
And they think the answer is beyond their grasp.
They can't find the answer without
the right information.
The problem is, they've left God out
of the human equation.
To find the answer, after all other avenues
have been explored,
doesn't a man have the right
to turn to the Lord?
He who put the stars and worlds into place
has the answer for the human race.

How to Find the Answer

So many people today are searching
for the answer to life's true meaning.
But they can only find it they have the right information,
and if they factor God into the human equation.
For too long God has been the unknown quantum.
They want to find the solution to their problem.
But they must look for it in the right places,
such as the books of the sacred pages.
To God's Word they are entitled to turn
for the answer they have yet to learn.
The answer is there for them to receive,
if they will only read it for themselves and believe.
It is us looking at a blind world with no way to get through.
We must help them see that the things most wonderful are true;
such as Heaven, with eternal youth and immortality;
God's forgiveness; and a life of joy for eternity.
We need to help these people see
how much better life in Christ can be.
If we show them certain Bible passages,
they would find out how loving and caring He is.
We could open the Bible and share with them
the solution to their problem.

Who Is Right?

Through life we each are on a journey
which will take us somewhere into eternity.
And for each of us, only two destinies are possible.
To cast aside this and other truth from the Bible
is the humanist's hidden objective.
They teach there are no absolutes, that it's all relative.
They have turned around the moral value system
to the extent that bad is considered good to them.
The old fashioned values, they say,
have no place in the world of today.
They don't even know why we should
live by what is decent and good.
No matter what they say to twist your mind,
the fact remains they are spiritually blind;
so they cannot see the right way.
The Lord knows what's best for you, do they?
Should you really trust their judgment over His?
What they tell you is not the way it really is.

Isn't It Silly?

Isn't it silly how we can have an energy shortage,
when every molecule has an immense power storage?

Isn't it stupid that the patent office will not grant a patent
for perpetual motion, because they say it's impossible to invent?

Isn't it silly that they hold to such a notion,
when atoms and star systems are perfect examples of perpetual motion?

Isn't it weird
how closed minds interfered
when someone had the answer all along?

Isn't it strange
that man doesn't change
his opinions, even when they're proven wrong?

Isn't it odd
that men don't want God
to save their souls, even though they wind up six feet beneath the sod?

Is The Day For Miracles Over?

The leaders of some churches say that the day
for miracles is over.
But they can't show you even one verse of
Scripture to prove it.
Some of us pray for the sick and they are healed;
true words of knowledge are revealed;
Those of us like Karl, who have spiritual vision,
really do see into the spiritual dimension;
A child like dear little Kelsey
writes down some true words of prophecy;
and Brenda speaks forth what's yet to come.
The unbeliever, of course, says it can't be done.
But still today God performs wonders
among His faithful followers.
When we extend hands of compassion,
something powerful starts to happen.
We reach out to people to bless or to heal,
and they can see that the power of God is real.
We give Him all the credit and glory
for the answers to prayer which we see;
for the great things He inspires us to do;
and for the miracles of healing, too.
That inspires faith in those who doubt.
Faith is what it's really all about.
Faith to see into the spiritual dimension –
faith to believe miracles still happen.

Do you have this faith?

In Defense of Our Faith

When we look at society as it is today,
we can see that man does not follow God's way.
It's time that the world pays heed
to the hallowed path that leads
people back to God and His way.
So many are led astray
by every wind that blows.
Religion is as religion goes.
Most religions are based on lies,
such as, getting ten virgins after one dies.
Christianity is based on historical fact.
But unbelievers don't want to hear that.
They mock the Christian religion.
They say it's just superstition.
Yet it's founded on <u>real</u> historical events.
It's the only religion which actually makes sense.
Whether Christ really lived is no big mystery.
It's on record. It's a matter of history.
The heathen can't discuss this in a cool-headed way.
They use anger to get across what they want to say.
I use simple logic that the truth may be seen,
and that people may understand what I mean.
The real truth is known by us, but not by them.
They can challenge our belief system,
but we aren't allowed to challenge theirs!
That sounds like a sorry state of affairs!
If you said that a lost soul needs a Savior,
they might explode in a burst of anger.
But there's no valid reason
to have such a strong emotional reaction.
Bursts of anger when there's no valid basis for it,
shows that one is emotionally ill and mentally unfit.
Their condition could be cured easily
by that humble Man of Galilee.
They must swallow their pride, repent and pray
that He would take their MADNESS away.

Who Is He?

Who is this man we find in God's Word
who claims to be "not of this world"?
He's not a character found in mythology,
because His life is a matter of history.
His birth was depicted in the constellations.
His life was foretold with exact specifications.
He came teaching truth, healing and bringing salvation
to save people from the pit of Satan.
He took on Himself our punishment to save us;
and while He was dying, He forgave us.
Because He was a god, He could not remain dead.
That's why He regained His life, and was resurrected.
The fact that He arose proved His deity.
It turns out, He really was who He claimed to be.
That humble man of Galilee
turns out to be the central figure in human history,
and the King of a vast celestial kingdom.
From His kingdom in Heaven, He left His throne
to be the most shining example of altruism
the world has ever known.
He has all power in the heavens and on Earth.
He is the King of the Universe,
and countless worlds are under His sovereignty.
He is the God of the gods. They worship Him and should not we?
Nehemiah 9:6: "The host of the heavens worships thee."

A Message From the King

I

It is my honor and privilege to bring
a message to you from the King.
Here's what He wants to tell you today:
Accept my love and believe what I say.
I freely offer to you and to everyone
my love, my forgiveness and my salvation.

II

When I first called man to walk with Me
along the path of light and beauty,
he chose darkness over light,
he chose wrong over what is right.
And still today, man chooses the same things,
in spite of all the harm and disappointment it brings.
He follows his own path, which leads to a pit.
Continuously, he keeps falling into it.
If one would follow Me, he would turn from the way he takes.
Generation after generation, man makes the same mistakes.
After thousands of years of stumbling, man does not learn,
because he chooses to follow the same pattern.
Instead of the things that are most wonderful,
he chooses the pleasures that are harmful,
and many pursuits that are passing,
instead of the good that is lasting.
These things create in the heart so much emptiness,
a life that is hollow and full of sadness.
Only I can fill the deep void in the heart of man,
yet he rejects Me time and time again.

III

I AM a king. I have called people to serve Me,
that they may feel useful, fulfilled and happy.
And yet, those on Earth are overwhelmed with violence and upheaval.
Everywhere we look, there is misery and so much evil.
And still man can't see the better way to live.
He refuses My way in spite of all that I offer to give.
I AM concerned about life on this planet today.
People need to see that there is a better way.
If man does not change the current trend,
life on Earth will come to an end.
Must their world come to an end before they find
that new beginning I have for mankind?
Must people be hit with disaster before they repent?

IV

I AM the One the Father has sent.
People look to Me as their Savior, King and confidante.
They ask, and I help them in distress, peril and want.
When you have such needs, you think I wouldn't care
about you, your life and your personal welfare.
Among billions, it would seem I could never get to you,
because after all, I have a vast kingdom to attend to.
But as a ruler, I manage to delegate authority
to the many leagues of angels serving under Me.
Yet even they are not enough. I need you
to do the work my angels do not do,
and to make sure my message gets through.

V

My Father grows impatient with the wickedness of man.
Soon the time will come when I shall walk the Earth again.
Until then, I will need you to be there for Me;
to carry my light into the darkness for all to see
and to go where I do not go.
So I call upon you now, as I've called the disciples long ago.

VI

My words in books and songs have been so widely used,
yet to many, my message is clouded and confused.
I will need you to make my message clear.
Your words of love will be as jewels for them to hear.
I will need you to say what needs to be said,
and to revive those who are spiritually dead.
My gift of salvation should be gladly received.
So often it is not, because so many are deceived.
Oh dear servant, help save my loved ones before they die.
You need more time to do this, and so do I.
If I were to call my sheep this night, few would come.
So I ask you to bring them into my Kingdom.

VII

Great evil has come into the world, which nothing can undo,
until I return to Earth and make all things new.
Spiritual darkness over the Earth fast approaches.
It will last until the light of a new dawn arises.
This will be the dawn of the Eternal Day.
The day of man will end and pass away.

VIII

Yet a little while, and back to your planet I will go,
to defend the city I left so long ago.
When the desolation of Jerusalem is nigh,
then the sign of the Son of Man will appear in the sky.
The forces which fight my angels will fall,
and I'll be victorious over them all.
All the governments of Earth shall surrender.
Then I will abolish war forever.
The world will see the end of the rule of man
when my Kingdom is established on Earth again.
With a rod of iron, I will rule over every nation
just as it was foretold in the Book of Revelation.
And during my thousand year reign,
I will elevate human life to a higher plane.

IX

The perfection of beauty will shine in life again,
and people will see my better way for man.
Then man will finally learn to follow my way,
and the sins of the world will be washed away.
For my people, all the problems of life will be gone.
At last the Day of Jubilee will dawn.
At that time, the glory of my Kingdom will be shown,
for there will be joy beyond all that man has known.

X

On that day, I will open the Door to Eternity,
and give each of my followers immortality.
At a time when science and faith become as one,
the tie that binds men to Earth shall be undone.
And just before man crosses the starry clime,
he will break through the barriers of light and time.
On that day, I'll bring down the Watchers from afar,
and give to man the bright morning star.
Countless worlds are under my sovereignty.
I AM in charge of the hosts of the heavens, which extend into infinity.